Perception and Representation

WITHDRAWN

Open Guides to Psychology

Series Editor: Judith Greene, Professor of Psychology at the Open University

Titles in the series

Learning to Use Statistical Tests in Psychology
Judith Greene and Manuela D'Oliveira

Basic Cognitive Processes
Judith Greene and Carolyn Hicks

Memory: A Cognitive Approach
Gillian Cohen, Michael W. Eysenck and Martin E. Le Voi

Language Understanding: A Cognitive Approach
Judith Greene

Problem Solving: A Cognitive Approach
Hank Kahney

Perception and Representation: A Cognitive Approach
Ilona Roth and John P. Frisby

Titles in preparation

Designing and Reporting Experiments
Peter Harris

Issues in Brain and Behaviour
Frederick Toates

Basic Social Psychology
Dorothy Miell

Perception and Representation: A Cognitive Approach

Parts I and II
by Ilona Roth

Part III
by John P. Frisby

Open University Press
Milton Keynes · Philadelphia

Open University Press
12 Cofferidge Close
Stony Stratford
Milton Keynes MK11 1BY, England

and
1900 Frost Road, Suite 101
Bristol, PA19007, USA

First published 1986. Reprinted 1989

British Library Cataloguing in Publication Data

Roth, Ilona
  Perception and representation: a cognitive
  approach. — (Open guides to psychology)
  1. Perception
  I. Title   II. Frisby, John P.   III. Series
  153.7   BF311

  ISBN 0-335-15328-3

Library of Congress Cataloging in Publication Data

Roth, Ilona.
  Perception and representation.

  (Open guides to psychology series)
  Bibliography: p.
  Includes indexes.
  1. Perception 2. Cognition. I. Frisby, John P.
II. Title.   III. Series.
BF311.R655   1986   153.7   85-21649

  ISBN 0-335-15328-3

Phototypeset by Dobbie Typesetting Service, Plymouth, Devon.
Printed in Great Britain at the Alden Press, Oxford.

*Parts I and II of this book are
dedicated to Benjamin and Jessica*

Perception and Representation: A Cognitive Approach

Contents

Part II   An Introduction to Object Perception

Ilona Roth

Part III The Computational Approach to Vision

John P. Frisby

Preface

Within the Open Guides to Psychology series, *Perception and Representation: A Cognitive Approach* is one of a companion set of four books, the others being *Language Understanding: A Cognitive Approach*; *Memory: A Cognitive Approach*; and *Problem Solving: A Cognitive Approach*. Together these form the main texts of the Open University third level course in Cognitive Psychology, but each of the four volumes can be read independently. The course is designed for second or third year students. It is presented in the style and format that the Open University has found to be uniquely effective in making the material intelligible and interesting.

The books provide an up-to-date and in-depth treatment of the major issues, theories and findings in cognitive psychology. They are designed to introduce a representative selection of different research methods, and the reader is encouraged, by means of Activities and Self-assessment Questions interpolated throughout the text, to become involved in cognitive psychology as an active participant.

The authors gratefully acknowledge the many helpful comments and suggestions of fellow members of the course team on earlier drafts, and the valuable assistance of Pat Vasiliou, Doreen Warwick and Ortenz Rose in typing the manuscript. In addition, Ilona Roth gratefully acknowledges the contribution of Gillian Cohen in helping to prepare Section 7 of Part II of this book; John Frisby gratefully acknowledges the many and varied contributions of John Mayhew over many years to his appreciation of the computational approach to vision, and warmly thanks Stephen Pollard for patient preparation of the computer-generated images.

Acknowledgements

Grateful acknowledgement is made to the following sources for material used in this pack:
Figures 2.1, 2.3 and 2.20 Carelman, J. (1971). *Catalogue of Extraordinary Objects* (translated by Rosaleen Walsh) Abelard-Schuman.

Introduction

The theme of this book is how we make sense of all the information we receive from the physical world. The world as we experience it is divided into relatively discrete structures. We are aware of objects, animals, plants etc. having particular sizes, shapes, colours and locations. Some of these things are stationary, others move as part of complex event sequences. Each has a specific function or significance. These physical things feature prominently in both our moment-to-moment perceptions of the world and the more permanent representations of the world which are stored as knowledge in memory. Each Part of the book adopts a different approach to explaining how such perceptions and representations are achieved. Certain major issues re-emerge in each Part.

Part I of the book is concerned with the concepts or conceptual categories which serve to organize our knowledge of the world into manageable chunks. These conceptual categories represent the shared characteristics by which individually different 'things' can be grouped together and differentiated from other groupings. They are fundamental to all cognitive activity, since without them perception, memory, language and all thought processes would be impossibly unwieldy. Much of the discussion is concerned with alternative conceptions of the nature of these mental representations. A contrast is drawn between the 'traditional' view that they are well-defined, clearly differentiated groupings of things, and the more recent idea that they are rather ill-defined fuzzy groupings of things. One conclusion which emerges is that different concept representations may be required for different classes of item, or for the same class of items under different circumstances.

Part II of the book considers how we actually see and recognize the objects which our conceptual categories serve to represent mentally. That is, how is the information received by the visual sense organs transformed into perceptions of objects with specific properties, functions and meanings? Much of the discussion is concerned with the processes which carry out this transformation. But for objects to be seen and recognized these processes must interact with previously stored conceptual knowledge. The nature of stored representations for object categories is therefore a continuing theme in this second part and some different approaches to their interaction with perceptual processes are illustrated.

Though many of the studies discussed in Part II are based on experiments, some workers have favoured the alternative approach of programming a computer to 'see' or 'recognize' objects. One merit of this approach is that the processes and representations which carry out a perceptual task are well understood since they are chosen by the person designing the system. However, the early computer vision systems described in this Part achieved only modest success.

The late David Marr has argued that the problem with both experimental and early computer studies of visual perception lies in their chosen level of explanation. More specifically, they have attempted to describe the processes and representations responsible for perception without adequately specifying the overall visual functions which they must achieve. Marr's philosophy of levels of explanation is introduced in Part II. Part III describes what the application of this philosophy has achieved in the field of artificial vision. The particular merit of Marr's approach is that it recognizes the complexity of the inputs which are processed in perception, and of the outputs which are achieved. However, neither Marr nor anyone else has yet designed a system which matches the apparently effortless way in which we see, recognize and interact with the complex world around us.

The coverage in this volume is necessarily limited. The discussion deals almost exclusively with the perception and representation of physical entities. Yet many of our perceptions and much of our stored knowledge is structured into much more abstract categories such as happiness, beauty, greed, etc. Though there has been research on this sort of problem, it has proved even more difficult to identify the criteria by which we decide that someone is happy or beautiful, than to identify those by which we decide that an object is a chair or a table. It is hoped, however, that theories dealing with concrete domains offer some insight for the perception and representation of more abstract domains.

A second limitation is that the discussion concentrates mainly on the visual modality. Yet much of our experience of the world comes through other modalities such as hearing. The criteria by which we decide that a particular 'thing' is a dog may include not only its appearance, but its smell, and the sound it makes. The studies of concept representation discussed in Part I do make some reference to these multiple modalities, but few studies of visual perception have attempted to handle its interaction with other modalities.

How to use this guide

In this book the reader will find Self-assessment Questions (SAQs) inserted at various points in the text. These SAQs provide the reader with a means of checking his or her understanding. The answers can be found at the end of the book and will help to illuminate points made in the text. Answering the SAQs engages the reader as an active participant rather than as just a passive recipient.

Detailed accounts of experiments are presented in Techniques Boxes and these are chosen as illustrative of representative experimental methods. The Summaries recapitulate the main points in each section and provide a useful aid to revision. The Index of Concepts that appears at the end of the book allows the reader to locate the place in the text where a concept is first introduced and defined. Entries in the Index of Concepts are italicized in the text.

Each part concludes with a short list of recommended further reading. Obviously the interested reader can also follow up the references given in the text. Some of these references are to articles in *Issues in Cognitive Modeling*, edited by Aitkenhead and Slack, which is the Reader for the Open University course in Cognitive Psychology. This is designed to be a companion volume to the other Cognitive Psychology volumes in the Open Guides to Psychology series.

Finally, the reader may wish to note that Parts I and II aim for fairly broad coverage of fundamental material, whereas Part III is a more technical treatment of a specific approach.

Part I
Conceptual Categories

Ilona Roth

Part I   Conceptual Categories

Contents

1   Introduction

One of the most important characteristics of cognition is that objects, entities and events, though individually different, are treated in thought and language as members of *conceptual categories*. The concept 'chair' for instance, is a mental grouping of objects which are individually different, but which tend to share certain characteristics in common. *Concepts* or conceptual categories, then, are *mental representations* of objects, entities or events, stored in memory.

Why is the ability to categorize such an integral and central part of cognition? Try to imagine a world in which we did not treat objects such as chairs as members of conceptual categories. One problem is that each object which we in fact perceive or 'see as' a chair would be seen as a novel object — we would be unable to *recognize* or *make sense* of such perceptions because we would have no common label to attach to them. Thus the ability to place objects in conceptual categories is a fundamental property of *perception*.

A second difficulty is that we would not know what to *do* with any new 'chair' we encountered, e.g. that it could be sat on. We understand about the function of chairs because this is part of the conceptual knowledge we have of that class of objects. Without this knowledge we would be unable to use or interact appropriately with 'chairs'. It can be concluded that the ability to categorize is essential for *action* — our responses to and interactions with the objects, entities and events which make up our world.

Memory, too, would function inefficiently without the ability to organize the knowledge we acquire into meaningful categories. We would be forced to store trivial information such as the details of each chair we had come across, instead of retaining only essential information such as the characteristics of chairs in general, and relevant knowledge about personally important chairs (my own armchair, the baby's high chair).

Finally, without conceptual categories, it would be extremely difficult to *communicate* about objects such as chairs. If we wanted to tell someone that we had just seen a chair, we would have to laboriously describe all the individual parts of the object, rather than simply denoting them by the single word 'chair'. Communication would become totally unwieldy. In short, conceptual categorization is central to all our cognitive abilities. As some writers have aptly put it: 'Concepts are the coinage of thought' (Johnson-Laird and Wason, 1977).

There is a particularly close and intricate connection between concepts and the words used to express them. For instance, 'chair' is both a concept and a word in our language—so can the two really be distinguished? Theoretically, the concept 'chair' is an abstract representation of the class of objects in question, stored in memory. In contrast, the word 'chair' is what we utter or write when referring to this class of objects. Experiments with organisms having no language, e.g. pigeons or young children, suggest that they can respond systematically to classes of objects such as red or square shapes. Presumably they are able to form abstract representations or concepts of these classes even though they cannot talk about them. On the other hand an adult's mental representation for 'chair' may take a verbal form. It follows that the relationship between conceptual categorization and language is a complex one. It has generated a great deal of empirical research but this is beyond the scope of the present discussion.

Before proceeding further, it is necessary to clarify how the important new terms introduced in this section will be used throughout the ensuing discussion. The terms *concept* and *conceptual category* will be used interchangeably to refer to mental representations of objects, entities and events. The term *categorization* will be used to describe the mental activity of grouping like things together into conceptual categories. Two other terms—*class* and *classification*—are roughly synonymous with 'conceptual category' and 'categorization'.

Summary of Section 1

- A concept or conceptual category is a mental representation of a set of objects, events or entities.
- The ability to group individually different items into conceptual categories according to their shared characteristics is central to all cognitive activities including perception, action, memory and communication.
- Concepts may be distinguished from the words which express them, though there is a close connection between the two.

2   Which concepts and why?

2.1   Perceived world structure

By treating objects, entities and events as members of conceptual categories, we are mentally dividing the world into distinct chunks. In this way we impose a *structure* on the world. But what accounts for the particular structure we impose? Consider conceptual categories such as 'rose', 'tulip' and 'pansy'. These categories serve to group together flowers sharing similar arrangements of sepals, petals, leaves etc. The groups so formed may include flowers of many different colours. Why then do we categorize flowers in this way, and not according to what colour they are? In short, what accounts for the particular conceptual categories people form?

One view of this, popular among anthropologists, has been expressed as follows:

> . . . the physical and social environment of the young child is perceived as a continuum. It does not contain any intrinsically separate 'things'. The child, in due course, is taught to impose upon this environment a kind of discriminating grid which serves to distinguish the world as being composed of a large number of separate things; each labelled with a name. (Leach, 1964)

According to this view, there is no basis for our category structure in the world itself. Instead this structure is imposed by categorical processes of the human mind, which in turn depend upon experiences within a particular culture. Thus the categories we use to distinguish varieties of flowers are simply those used by other members of our culture. Clearly this is true of some conceptual categories. For instance, we often think of species of flowers such as snowdrop, daffodil, as members of a common category of plants which grow from bulbs. In another culture which uses plants for medicinal purposes, the same species may be treated as separate categories because each has different medicinal properties.

Anthropologists have described many phenomena of this kind, and some have concluded that culture is the source for *all* of the conceptual categories with which we structure the world. However, in the recent work of psychologists on how we categorize, a different emphasis has emerged: 'The world *does* contain "intrinsically separate things".' These are 'information-rich bundles of perceptual and functional attributes . . . that form natural discontinuities' (Rosch *et al.*, 1976).

In contrast to Leach, Rosch is saying that the world already comes with structure, and this affects the categorical processes of the human mind. According to this view, it is not merely an accident of culture that we categorize flowers as we do. It is because particular arrangements of petals, sepals, leaves, etc. frequently occur together in the living world. Similarly, wings tend to occur with feathers, rather than with fur, though there are exceptions in animals such as bats and flying squirrels. Lungs tend to be found in animals which live on land, though again there are exceptions in animals such as lung fish. Among inanimate objects, those used for sitting on tend to have four legs supporting a flat surface, though there are examples with three, one or even no legs. In short, there are *natural correlations* among the properties of things in our world such that they frequently, though not invariably go together.

The structure of our mental representations comes both from these correlations of properties, and also from the machinery with which we perceive them. For instance, there are specialized regions of certain flower petals which reflect ultra-violet light. Insects which can see ultra-violet light use these markings to guide them to honey sources within the flowers. It is as if the insects treat flowers having this property as members of a common category of honey sources. Because the human visual system is not sensitive to ultra-violet light, we do not generally categorize flowers according to whether or not they reflect ultra-violet light. In this way our perceptual mechanisms help to determine which aspects of real world structure are represented in our category system. The categories we form are those which represent the natural correlational structure of the world, further shaped by the mechanisms with which we perceive it. Rosch has termed this the principle of *perceived world structure*. Notice, however, that the ultra-violet reflecting properties of flowers are known to us via scientific measuring devices, and so may become part of the classificatory system which botanists use for flowers. Scientific observations frequently suggest new ways of structuring the world which add to, or even replace, our 'direct' perceptual categorizations.

2.2   Cognitive economy

Rosch goes on to argue that the role of the human category system is to reflect perceived world structure in a set of categories which provide maximum information with minimum effort. For instance, we do not (generally speaking) treat chairs made of wood, metal and plastic as separate categories, because these distinctions are not very useful in recognizing, thinking about, and discussing chairs. On the other hand, it *is* useful to distinguish between chairs and tables because there is an important difference in their function—chairs are for sitting on, tables are for putting things on. Generally speaking, the categories we form are designed to minimize cognitive effort by taking advantage of perceived world structure and representing it in the most 'economical' way. This is known as the principle of *cognitive economy*.

2.3   Shareability constraints

On the surface, the anthropological view with which we commenced this section conflicts with that of Rosch and other contemporary psychologists. The first emphasizes culture as the source for all our conceptual categories, whereas the second emphasizes structure inherent in our world and our perception of it. However, these factors must interact with each other to some extent. For instance, I mentioned that we do not generally treat chairs made of different materials as separate categories, but a specialist such as a cabinet-maker might do precisely that. Similarly, we do not perceive flowers which reflect ultra-violet light as members of a distinct category, but a botanist might classify them as such. Generally speaking, what may be an economical distinction for a set of individuals in one culture or subculture may not satisfy the requirements of others. In this way cultural factors must play a part in determining what categories are developed by different individuals, social groups or societies.

The real problem, then, is to determine how cultural forces interact with the structured nature of objects and events in the world, and the processing that takes place by the perceiver. An important consideration (Freyd, 1983) is that the categories formed by a particular social group must be capable of being shared by all members of that group. Hence the potential structuring capacity of the mind will be constrained by the requirement that categories are *shareable*, i.e. make sense to more than one individual. For instance, in a culture such as our own in which cutlery is used for consuming food, concepts such as knife, fork, spoon may be easily represented and communicated: they are shareable. However, in a culture in which food is consumed with the fingers, the concepts of knife, fork and spoon could not be easily represented or communicated. This suggests that a third principle—that of *shareability constraints*—affects how we categorize.

Summary of Section 2

- The conceptual categories we form are partly determined by the structured nature of our world, and by our perceptual mechanisms. This is known as the principle of *perceived world structure*.
- Conceptual categories serve to represent perceived world structure with maximum information and minimum effort. This is known as the principle of *cognitive economy*.
- Culture plays a part in determining which categories meet the requirements of cognitive economy. The categories which are formed must be capable of being shared between members of a cultural group. This is known as the principle of *shareability constraints*.

3   *The nature of concepts*

We will conduct a simple exercise designed to give us some insights into the way we think about particular conceptual categories. Imagine that you are asked to explain what is meant by a concept such as 'table' to someone who is unfamiliar with this type of object — perhaps a child or a member of a completely different culture. You would try to give a description of the shared identifying characteristics of tables by which the person might recognize one. We will try this exercise with three different types of concept, starting with a mathematical concept.

3.1   *A mathematical concept*

Activity 1
Using the guidelines just given, write down a description which characterizes the conceptual category 'triangle'. Cover up the remainder of the page while you write down your answer.

My answer looks like this:
(a) 2-dimensional geometric figure
(b) Has three straight sides
(c) Sides are joined to each other at their ends
(d) Has angles adding up to 180°
(e) Different types:
   Equilateral (three equal sides)
   Isosceles (two equal sides)
   Right-angled (one angle of 90°)
The content of your answer was probably very similar to mine if, like me, you based it on your recollections of school geometry. However, if you have ever specialized in mathematics, you may have included additional or alternative characteristics. Individuals' mental representations of concepts such as 'triangle' share much in common — as we have already mentioned, communication would be difficult if they did not. At the same time, there are some differences, for which expert or specialist knowledge is a particularly powerful source.

You may of course have organized the information differently from me. You may even have included a sketch based on your *mental image* of a triangle. These different ways of externalizing the information suggest that there may be different ways of organizing it in our minds, though we should not assume a direct correspondence between what we write down and the mental organization of the information.

In my list for 'triangle', each item refers to a *property* commonly associated with triangles. You will come across this term frequently in the forthcoming discussion, along with two related terms—*attribute* and *feature*. The three terms are more or less interchangeable, though some psychologists reserve the term 'feature' for specific types of property—such as the parts which make up a triangle.

Looking more closely at the individual properties listed for 'triangle', item (a) '2-dimensional geometric figure' shows that we may think of the category 'triangle' as belonging to a more general category which implicitly includes other categories such as 'quadrilateral' and 'pentagon'. Thus geometric figures are thought of as belonging to a common *superordinate* category. At the same time, the different types of triangle listed under (e) indicate that we may differentiate the category 'triangle' into smaller groupings—equilateral, isosceles, etc. These are *subordinate* categories of the concept 'triangle'. All this information may be represented in the form of a diagram.

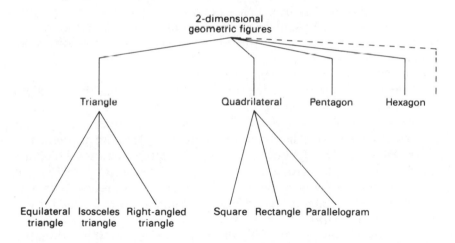

Figure 1.1 A hierarchical organization for two-dimensional geometric figures

Figure 1.1 is a way of organizing information known as a *hierarchy*. The main principle of hierarchical organization is that a general or most inclusive category (the superordinate) appears at the top of the hierarchy. This superordinate category includes or subsumes more specific categories which appear at the next level down. At the bottom of the hierarchy are even more specific categories which are included within each of the intermediate level categories. These are the subordinate categories. The hierarchy thus shows all the relationships between categories in a particular *domain*, in this case 2-dimensional geometric figures. In our example the hierarchy has just three levels, but in other domains categories may lend themselves to more complex hierarchies having many more levels.

The principle of hierarchical organization is employed in many fields in order to classify information. For instance, zoologists divide up the animal kingdom into classes or divisions ranging from the most general *phyla* such as chordates — animals having a bony tail at some stage during their life-cycle — down to individual species such as homo sapiens. The relationships of class inclusion are then represented in a hierarchy known as a *taxonomy*. This taxonomy is an example of a systematic classification — its details are agreed upon by members of the academic community as a result of scientific observation and debate. The hierarchy shown in Figure 1.1 is not necessarily a widely accepted representation of the relations among geometric figures. Indeed, it is a rather simplistic hierarchy, since for instance 'square' is technically a sub-category of 'rectangle', and no curved figures have been included. The real implication of including it here is to suggest that it reflects the way in which I personally represent information about 2-dimensional geometric figures in my mind. The ubiquity of hierarchical systems of classification in everyday life is surely an indication of how our minds work. Later in our discussion we will consider the empirical evidence for this viewpoint.

Referring again to our list for 'triangle', items (b) 'has three straight sides' and (c) 'sides are joined to each other at their ends' consist of *perceptual features* of triangles. These particular perceptual features are *visual* — what we can tell about triangles by looking at them. For other categories we might of course list perceptual features which are auditory, tactile, olfactory, etc. Item (d) 'angles add up to 180°' is also a property of triangles, but it is not perceptual — it is not something we could discover about triangles by looking at them. Instead it is a mathematical or *formal property*.

Notice that items (a), (b), (c) and (d) are properties of *all* triangles. Technically these properties are described as *necessary properties* of triangles, because a triangle cannot be a triangle unless it possesses them. However, not all of these four properties apply *only* to triangles. Item (a) and item (c) are also properties of all quadrilaterals, pentagons, etc. So if we want to describe triangles in a way which distinguishes them from these other figures, we must also take into account properties (b) and (d) — which apply only to triangles. If we now consider the combination of all four properties: '2-dimensional geometric figure, having three straight sides, joined at their ends, and angles adding up to 180°', we have a description which applies to all triangles and only triangles. Technically this description is said to be *necessary* and *sufficient* for the category 'triangle', because any figure which possesses this combination of properties is guaranteed to be a triangle. In practice this description serves as a *definition* of the category 'triangle' which clearly distinguishes it from other categories such as squares and rectangles, shoes and sausages!

Finally, notice that the items listed under (e) are *optional properties* of triangles. They are neither necessary nor sufficient for triangles so they do not form part of the definition of this concept.

SAQ 1
(a) The following list of properties is necessary for the category 'square', but it is not sufficient. Why?
  2-dimensional geometric figure
  Has four straight sides
  Sides are joined at their ends
  Angles add up to 360°
(b) What properties, if added, would convert the description into a set of necessary and sufficient properties which define the category 'square'?

It should be clear that it is possible to specify geometric figures such as triangles in terms of a combination of relatively few properties which apply exclusively to triangles. Another way of saying this is that we can specify a *conceptual rule* which will invariably identify triangles and distinguish them from non-triangles. The psychological implication is that a person's mental representation for 'triangle' may consist of a conceptual rule which defines this category. However, it does not necessarily follow that everyone will represent 'triangle' in this way.

3.2   An everyday concept

Now we will consider a different type of example—the category 'chair'.

Activity 2
Just as for Activity 1, see if you can write down a description which characterizes the category 'chair'. Cover up the rest of the page while you write your answer.

Your answer probably looks something like this:

(a) Item of furniture
(b) Used for sitting on
(c) Has flat horizontal surface
(d) Has four legs
(e) Has a straight back rest
(f) May have arms
(g) Different types, e.g. dining, kitchen.

In some ways this list resembles the one drawn up for 'triangle'. Item (a) provides a superordinate category which includes chair, table, desk and other categories of furniture. Item (g) gives examples of subordinate categories of chairs. So information about chairs, like triangles, can be represented as a hierarchy. Items (c), (d), (e) and (f) give perceptual features of chairs. Item (b), like item (d) in the 'triangle' list, is a non-perceptual property. In this case the property concerns the *function* of chairs. Such functional information seems to play an important part in specifying many categories of everyday objects.

An important consideration in comparing this list with the list for 'triangle' is whether any of the properties are necessary.

SAQ 2
Are there any properties in the list which an object *must* have to be a chair (i.e. necessary properties)?

The striking difference between the two lists is that though there are two (non-perceptual) properties which are necessary for chairs, there are a relatively large number of perceptual features none of which is truly necessary. For instance, though *many* chairs have a flat horizontal surface for sitting on, some have a sloping surface, some have a curved surface. Similarly, many chairs have four legs, but there are also chairs with three, one or even no legs. Similar exceptions can be found for items (e) and (f). Figure 1.2 shows just a few of the many objects which count as chairs. They are all clearly recognizable as chairs, and yet each of them is an exception to at least one of the properties on our list.

A second contrast between this and our 'triangle' list is that there is no combination of properties which appears to refer to all chairs and only chairs (i.e. necessary and sufficient properties). Thus, items (a) and (b) are necessary for chairs, but they also apply to seats, benches and stools so they are not sufficient for chairs. Even when we add properties (c), (d), (e) and (f), we still do not have a description which applies only to chairs.

SAQ 3
Why is the combination of properties (a) to (f) not sufficient to guarantee that an object is a chair?

You may find yourself disagreeing with some of my claims about the properties of chairs — but this is significant in itself! Whereas there seems little room for argument about what defines a triangle, it seems difficult to specify any combination of properties which will be generally agreed to constitute a definition of 'chair'. Only the superordinate category (furniture) and the function (for sitting on)

Figure 1.2   What is a chair? Each of these chairs has a different set of properties

clearly apply to all chairs but these properties also apply to several other categories. Perhaps then, chairs, unlike triangles, cannot be specified in terms of defining properties which apply to all chairs and only to chairs. In fact, there seems to be some overlap of properties between chairs and certain other categories of furniture. The psychological implication is that conceptual categories such as 'chair' are not mentally represented in terms of lists or properties which clearly define the categories and distinguish them from other categories. The representations for such categories are said to be *ill defined* and *fuzzy*.

An important clue to what these representations consist of is provided by the perceptual features which I have listed for chairs. Notice that (c), (d) and (e) are all features that we might associate with

29

a *typical* chair. Hence we might think of chairs as typically having four legs and a straight back rest, even though we know of exceptions. This suggests that our mental representation for classes of objects such as chair is based upon the characteristics of typical members of the class. Obviously this mental representation will not apply equally or fully to all members of the class. There will be some objects (the atypical ones) which share very little in common with the mental representation. This means that we may have difficulty in deciding whether they belong to the category or not. Look, for instance, at the example in Figure 1.3.

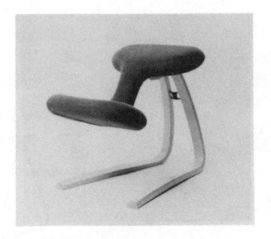

Figure 1.3   An atypical chair, known as a 'Balans' chair

Without the prior discussion you might have had difficulty deciding what this object was, though you would probably have recognized it as an item of furniture used for sitting on. Moreover, your decision might have been affected by *context*. For instance, as we have been talking about chairs you probably did classify the object as a chair. But if I had told you that it was used in classrooms you might have decided that it was a stool or seat. Clearly there is something fuzzy about the concept 'chair' if a particular object is included under some circumstances and excluded under others.

This contrast between the ways we have characterized triangles and chairs suggests that the conceptual categories which we form for different classes of objects or entities may be of different kinds. At least theoretically, geometric figures can be represented in terms of categories which are clear-cut and well-defined by a small number of necessary and sufficient properties. In contrast, items of furniture are more readily represented by conceptual categories which are fuzzy, being characterized rather than defined by numerous optional properties usually associated with typical members. An important question, to which we will return later in the discussion, is which other classes of objects or entities lend themselves to these two different modes of categorization? It is sometimes claimed that concepts in technical domains (e.g. science, law, mathematics) tend to be of the first well-defined kind, whereas our concepts of the objects and entities we encounter in everyday life (furniture, vehicles, clothing, etc.) are of the second fuzzy variety. There are other more complex possibilities, as our third and final example shows.

3.3   A biological concept

For this final example we will consider a conceptual category of living organisms — 'dog'.

SAQ 4
  (i) Following the same lines as in Activities 1 and 2, see if you can work out a description which characterizes the category 'dog'.
 (ii) Does your list include any properties/features which are necessary for the category 'dog'?
(iii) Does any combination of properties/features on your list apply only to dogs?
 (iv) Now try to imagine that you are a zoologist carrying out the same exercise. In what ways (if any) do you think your list for 'dog' might differ?

This final example makes clear that the same concept may be described in terms of two rather different lists of properties. Most people, if asked for an immediate rough-and-ready response to the question 'what is a dog?', would produce a rough-and-ready list of properties typically associated with dogs. A zoologist answering the same question might be able to produce a list of technical properties approximating a definition of the category.

The first type of list is similar to the one drawn up for 'chair'. It lacks a combination of features which applies to all dogs and only dogs and implies a mental representation which is somewhat fuzzy and ill-defined.

The second type of list resembles the list for 'triangles'. It is a combination of scientific properties which applies to virtually all dogs and to very few other organisms. It implies a clear-cut, well-defined representation.

These two different representations may even be held by the same person. For instance, a zoologist may have both a fuzzy representation of 'dog' which he uses for everyday purposes such as talking to his children, and a relatively clear-cut definition of 'dog' which he uses in scientific work. Even the layman does not in practice confuse dogs with cats, horses or other animals. Perhaps after all he does possess a clear representation of the category but one which is not readily expressed as a list of properties.

The notion of dual representations for the same concept seems particularly relevant for biological categories of animals and plants. However, it is quite possible that other types of categories—including triangles and chairs—have more than one representation! These are complex and important questions to which we will return in Section 7.

Summary of Section 3

- Relationships between conceptual categories may be mentally represented as hierarchies in which the most general superordinate categories include specific subordinate categories at lower levels.
- People associate properties, also known as attributes or features, with conceptual categories. Properties are of various kinds including perceptual, functional and formal ones.
- Necessary properties are ones which an item must have to be included in a particular category. A combination of necessary and sufficient properties is one which guarantees that an item is a member of a particular category—it defines the category.
- Conceptual categories which can be specified in terms of necessary and sufficient properties are clear-cut and well-defined. Categories without necessary and sufficient properties are ill-defined and fuzzy—sharing properties in common with other categories.
- Well-defined or fuzzy representations may be appropriate for different types of concept, or for the same concept under different circumstances.

4   Representations, processes and strategies: the old and the new

The activities carried out in the previous section raised some important questions about concepts. For instance, how are they specified? Are they characterized by hard and fast rules (all chairs have four legs) or rules of thumb (chairs usually have four legs)? What is the role of lists of properties in specifying concepts? Are these properties perceptual, functional, formal or of other more abstract kinds? In what way are the relationships between categories (e.g. between chairs and other items of furniture) specified? Are the same principles applicable to all categories, or different principles to different categories? In essence, all these questions are about people's representations for conceptual categories. Specifically, they concern the content and structure of these representations.

Another question, not yet touched upon, is how we decide to what category a particular item belongs. Given that we have concepts such as 'chair', 'bench' and 'stool' represented in memory, how do we decide on the appropriate categorization for a new object we encounter. This question concerns the *processes* by which particular objects, entities or events are assigned to appropriate categories.

Finally, we might ask how conceptual categories are *acquired* in the first place. For instance, how do we acquire the knowledge that enables us to classify and respond to objects such as chairs appropriately? In part this is a question about the cognitive development of children. Any of you who are familiar with children will have observed the gradual process by which they come to use terms such as 'chair' appropriately. Initially a child may use the term for several items of furniture and only gradually narrow it down to apply to that group of objects which we, as adults, classify as chairs. But *concept acquisition* is not only a phenomenon of childhood—it continues throughout adult life. Think of the *new* concepts which one acquires as one gets older: they range from concrete concepts such as the parts of a car or the ingredients of a dish to highly abstract concepts such as socialism or fashion. So concept acquisition is a central facet of both child development and adult cognition. The main focus of concern here is with the *strategies* used in acquiring new concepts.

To summarize, an understanding of how we categorize focuses upon three main issues:

1 *Representations:* How are conceptual categories mentally represented?
2 *Processes:* How are particular items assigned to these categories?
3 *Acquisition strategies:* How are these categories acquired?

Though all these questions seem of central importance to an understanding of conceptual categorization, they have not always been given equal emphasis in research. Pioneering work carried out in the 1950s and '60s by psychologists such as Bruner, was mainly concerned with an understanding of acquisition strategies. In more recent work, there has been a marked shift of emphasis away from the study of acquisition strategies towards the study of representations and, to some extent, processes. Exceptions to this trend are the studies of children where, for obvious reasons, acquisition strategies remain a major concern. In order to understand the shift in emphasis, we will first return to the classic studies carried out by Bruner.

4.1 Bruner's studies of acquisition strategies

Imagine that you want to investigate how everyday concepts such as 'chair' are initially acquired. It is obviously fruitless to ask adults how they learned them, since they are most unlikely to remember, and in any case introspections are not necessarily unreliable. It might seem easier to study children who are still in the process of acquiring these concepts, but this also poses problems. Children young enough to be still learning the concepts are even less able to introspect than adults and they may be unwilling to cooperate in experimental tasks. Developmental psychologists have found ways round these problems, but Bruner and his colleagues (Bruner, Goodnow and Austin, 1956) chose nonetheless to work with adults.

In order to provide novel concepts to be learned by adults, Bruner *et al.* made up their own. By combining familiar concepts such as 'red' and 'triangle' they produced arbitrary combinations which they specified as *conceptual rules* such as 'red triangle'. They also devised an experimental procedure for 'externalizing' people's mental processes (which they termed *strategies*) for acquiring these rules. Details of Bruner's studies are given in Techniques Box A.

TECHNIQUES BOX A

Studies of Concept Acquisition Strategies (e.g. Bruner *et al.* 1956)

Rationale
To study how people acquire new concepts, where these consist of artificial conceptual rules specified by an Experimenter (E).

Method
The people taking part in the experiment, i.e. the Subjects (Ss) were shown an array of items. Typically these consisted of simple geometric shapes drawn on cards and varying along three or four dimensions (termed *attributes* by Bruner). Figure 1.4 illustrates a simplified version of a typical array. There are 27 items made up from three *values* of each of three attributes. Attributes and their values are as follows:

Attribute	*Value*
Shape	Cross, circle, square
Number of shapes	One, two, three
Shading of shapes	Plain, filled, stippled

The Experimenter (E) made up a number of conceptual rules which applied to subsets of items in the array. For instance, the conceptual rule 'two circular shapes' applies to items 11, 14 and 17 which are termed

---

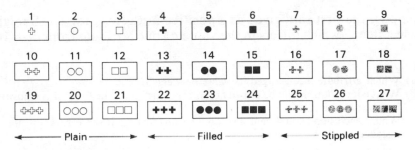

Figure 1.4   Simplified version of the array of items used in a Bruner task

positive instances of the rule. All remaining items in the array are non-instances of the rule. Notice that in this two-attribute rule, the third attribute, shading, is irrelevant.

Ss were first shown one positive instance of the E's conceptual rule. In order to discover the rule, Ss selected particular items one at a time from the array and were told whether or not they are instances of it. This continued until Ss could state the rule correctly. The E recorded the sequence of items chosen by each S.

Results
From the sequence of items selected by each S the E drew inferences about the different strategies used by Ss to acquire the conceptual rules. The number of selections taken to reach a solution also indicated which types of strategy were most successful. The main kinds of strategy are described below.

SAQ 5
(a) Suppose an E has formulated the conceptual rule 'plain squares'. Which two attributes are involved and which value of each?
(b) Now write down the numbers of all items in Figure 1.4 to which this rule applies (i.e. positive instances of the rule).

Bruner identified two main classes of acquisition strategies from Ss' response sequences in these studies.

Focusing strategies
The general principle of focusing strategies is that the S tests the *relevance* of attributes as a means of deducing the concept. The commonest version is *conservative focusing*. The S takes the first card given as a positive instance and chooses a sequence of further cards which vary just one attribute at a time in order to test the relevance of each attribute to the rule. Taking the array shown in Figure 1.4,

suppose the first card given as a positive instance is 16. The S might select item 7 which differs in the value of one attribute from item 16.

SAQ 6
(a) Which attribute has changed its value between 16 and 7?
(b) What conclusion should be drawn about this attribute if the E says 7 is a positive instance of the rule?
(c) What conclusion should be drawn about this attribute if the E says 7 is not an instance of the rule?

The choice of instance on the next trial is designed to test the relevance of one of the remaining attributes whose relevance is still in doubt. For instance, if the S has already established that number of shapes *is* relevant, he or she has to decide which of the other attributes — shape or shading — is part of the rule. The S proceeds by selecting instances to test the relevance of as many attributes as he needs to deduce the rule. Once he knows which attributes are relevant, he merely checks the specific values of these attributes present in the first positive instance, in order to state the rule. For instance, if the S started with item 16 and established that number of shapes and shading were relevant, he would know that the rule was 'two stippled shapes'.

A variant of this strategy is known as *focus gambling*. It involves varying the values of two or more attributes simultaneously in the hope of eliminating the irrelevant ones in fewer trials.

Scanning strategies
The main alternative to focusing strategies are scanning strategies. Instead of testing the relevance of attributes to the rule, the S formulates hypothetical rules which are consistent with the first positive instance given. In *successive scanning* the S tests one hypothetical rule at a time, by selecting instances which will be positive or negative if the rule is the correct one. He carries on testing one hypothesis until feedback from E indicates that it is not in fact the correct one. He then repeats this process with other hypotheses until, by eliminating the incorrect hypotheses, he knows what the correct rule is.

For instance, suppose again the item 16 is the first positive instance indicated by the E. As in our earlier discussion we will assume that just two of the three attributes are relevant in the rule. Each of the following rules applies to this instance and so could hypothetically be the correct one:

    stippled cross shape(s)

    two cross shapes

    two stippled shapes

SAQ 7
Suppose the S is testing the hypothesis 'two crosses'. Having been told that item 16
is positive, what should he conclude:
(a) If he selects item 13 and is told it is positive?
(b) If he selects item 13 and is told it is negative?
(c) If he selects item 14 and is told it is negative?

The main variant of the scanning strategy is *simultaneous scanning*,
in which alternative hypotheses are not tested in a strictly serial fashion.
Essentially, the S attempts to select instances which will simultaneously
test *all* hypotheses compatible with the original instance. He tries to
remember which hypotheses are ruled out by each positive and negative
instance he selects.

The main disadvantage of both types of scanning strategy is that
it is difficult for the S to remember which hypotheses have been proved
wrong and which remain to be tested. Simultaneous scanning, in
particular, places far too great a load on memory. Conservative
focusing is the most efficient of the four strategies in this sort of task.
It places a small load on the S's memory, since he only has to keep
track of one attribute at a time. It also guarantees that, on average,
the solution is reached in the least number of moves.

Though these strategies are theoretically quite distinct, it is not always
easy to work out which one a S is using from his response sequence.
Sometimes the same sequence of responses could reflect either
conservative focusing or successive scanning. Also, Ss may use a
mixture of strategies—fluctuating between them from one sequence
of responses to another.

4.2   Bruner's model of concept acquisition and representation

You may be wondering what Bruner's studies have to do with how
people acquire and represent concepts. Bruner presumably believed
that there is a parallel between the task carried out by his Ss, and the
real-life situation of people (children and adults) acquiring new
conceptual knowledge. He saw his experiments as a 'model' both of
how people acquire concepts and, implicitly, of what these concepts
are like.

Consider the example of a child who is learning the concept 'ball'.
On analogy with Bruner's experiments the child is in the position of
trying to work out a conceptual rule which defines what it is that
certain objects, referred to by adults as 'balls', share in common. Once
the child has acquired this knowledge he too should be able to use
the term 'ball' appropriately, i.e. for precisely that class of objects

which adults think of as balls. However, there are important differences between Bruner's task and the actual situation of a person learning a new concept. For one thing, in Bruner's task there are artificial constraints on the information available to the subject. The subject is obliged to make a series of guesses, and the feedback is carefully controlled—it consists of just 'yes' and 'no' responses to these guesses. This is quite unlike the situation of the child (or for that matter adult) who is learning a new concept—many types of information will be available and many types of feedback given. Just think of the many types of feedback you give deliberately or accidentally to a child learning a new concept such as ball ('Give me the ball.' 'No, that's not the ball—that's an orange.' 'Where is your ball?' 'There it is.' 'Show me the picture of the ball.' 'Yes, that's it.' . . .).

Another artificial feature of Bruner's task is that the S is presented with a whole array of items which remain in front of him while he works out what the conceptual rule is. In everyday life this almost never happens. My daughter, aged sixteen months, sometimes points to a ball and gives it its correct name. On other days she points to the sun using the same name. Unlike the S in Bruner's experiment, she cannot look to and fro from ball to sun to work out where she has 'gone wrong'. Unless ball and sun happen to be present at the same moment, she must rely on her memory of the attributes which differ between the two. Because Bruner's tasks are so artificial they may induce strategies which are quite unlike those used by people (adults or children) acquiring new concepts in everyday life. So Bruner's studies may be misleading as a general model of acquisition strategies—which is, after all, what he was attempting to describe.

A final criticism of Bruner's model concerns his underlying assumptions about how concepts are mentally represented. He formulated his experimental concepts in terms of conceptual rules defined by attribute values. The implication is quite clearly that concepts are represented, like the triangles in Activity 1, as lists of properties or features, these feature lists being necessary and sufficient for the concepts in question. In fact Bruner's model is sometimes described as a *feature model*.

The problem with these assumptions is that though they were true, by definition, of Bruner's artificial concepts, he made no effort to test their validity for more realistic concepts. In practice, as we saw in Section 3, there are problems in generalizing the notion of necessary and sufficient defining features to everyday concepts such as 'chair', or even biological concepts such as 'dog'.

These criticisms show how a particular methodology—in this case, laboratory experiment—may place constraints upon theory. The outcome is an approach which lacks what is called *ecological validity*.

Because the approach is tailor-made for the laboratory, it fails to generalize to the everyday cognitive activities which it is meant ultimately to explain. Later studies of conceptual classification attempted to devise more naturalistic tasks and used everyday concepts as materials. This emphasis upon a more ecologically valid approach was the main reason why interest shifted from the study of acquisition strategies to mental representations of concepts. Once psychologists started to study everyday concepts, they were forced to confront the problem of how these concepts are mentally represented. In so doing, they cast doubt on the traditional assumption of rule-like representations.

Interestingly, there is a hint of this shift even in the work of Bruner and his associates. In some studies using rather more realistic stimuli (such as pictures of aircraft), Ss had to deal with attribute values which, unlike defining properties, did not invariably go with a particular concept — so-called *probabilistic cues*. There is, then, some hint that the structure required to represent conceptual categories may not always conform to Bruner's original view. It is this theme which dominated later work, notably by the psychologist Eleanor Rosch.

4.3   Conceptual hierarchies in semantic memory

We will mention one other landmark in the shift towards an ecologically valid theory of representation. This is Collins and Quillian's (1969) model of how information is stored and processed within semantic memory.

Collins and Quillian broke with the tradition of studying artificial concepts by investigating how people mentally represent information about biological classes such as birds, fish and mammals and everyday categories such as types of drink. They proposed that such information is represented by hierarchies similar to those discussed in Section 3.1. The general principles of their model are illustrated in Figure 1.5 which shows Collins and Quillian's version of a zoological taxonomy. At the top of the hierarchy are broad general categories, known as superordinates, in this case *animals*. These break down into more specific categories such as *mammals*, *birds*, *fish*. These in turn break down into even more specific categories, e.g. canaries, ostriches. At each level in the hierarchy, the categories are linked to a list of properties such as 'eats' or 'has feathers'. The more general superordinate categories are linked to a list of general properties which are shared by all category members. Categories at lower levels link only to special properties which are not generally applicable. For instance, the representation for the category 'bird' consists of features

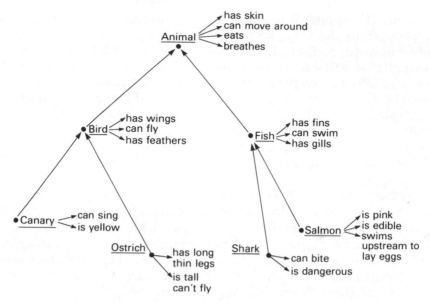

Figure 1.5   Part of Collins and Quillian's hierarchy for animals

such as 'has wings', 'can fly', which are not listed for the superordinate 'animal', since they apply only to birds. These features are assumed to apply to all birds, with exceptions such as that ostriches can't fly listed at the level below. This is an elegant way of achieving 'cognitive economy' (see Section 2.2), since it means that a property such as 'can fly' is only listed once — for birds — and not for each individual type of bird.

Notice that though this model represents the relationships between categories as a hierarchy, it makes assumptions similar to Bruner's about how *individual* concepts are represented. Firstly, category representations are assumed to consist of lists of properties or features. Secondly, a combination of these properties is assumed to apply to all category members and only category members — and thus define the category. There is, however, the qualification that individual category members such as ostrich may be specifically excepted from the defining rule.

Finally, the model specifies processes by which information can be retrieved from the hierarchy. Suppose that someone is trying to work out whether a statement such as 'a canary is an animal' is true. In order to verify this statement, the person must locate the relevant category (i.e. 'animal') and decide whether canary is a member of it. As Figure 1.5 shows, this requires a search through two levels in the hierarchy. On the other hand, if the statement to be verified is 'a canary is a bird' the relevant category is only one level away. Collins and Quillian argued that since Ss need time to search through the hierarchy, the first statement should take longer to verify than the second. Similarly, if Ss are asked to verify statements such as 'a canary can breathe' this should take longer than 'a canary has wings'. Likewise, 'property' statements should take longer to verify than 'category' statements, since the S must retrieve a property ('has wings') as well as locating the category which possesses this property. In order to test their model, Collins and Quillian used a task known as *sentence verification* as shown in Techniques Box B.

TECHNIQUES BOX B

Sentence Verification Experiments (Collins and Quillian, 1969)

Rationale
To investigate the times taken to verify statements about animals. If categories are organized hierarchically, it should take longer to deal with sentences involving category information from non-adjacent levels. In addition, sentences about properties of animals should take longer to verify than sentences about category membership.

Method
Ss were asked to decide whether presented sentences are true or false. Sentences involved either no-level, one-level or two-level searches, and could be of two main types: *category verification* or *property verification* (see Table 1).

Table 1

Category verification	Property verification	No. of levels
A canary is a canary	A canary can sing	0
A canary is a bird	A canary has wings	1
A canary is an animal	A canary has skin	2
A canary is a fish	A canary has gills	False

Sentences like these were displayed one at a time on a screen and reaction times were measured between the onset of the sentence and the subject pressing a 'true' or 'false' button.

Results
Figure 1.6 shows that the mean times taken by Ss to verify sentences (vertical axis) depended on the number of levels which must be searched (horizontal axis). In addition, the 'property' sentences took longer than the 'category' sentences. This is consistent with the hierarchical model proposed by Collins and Quillian.

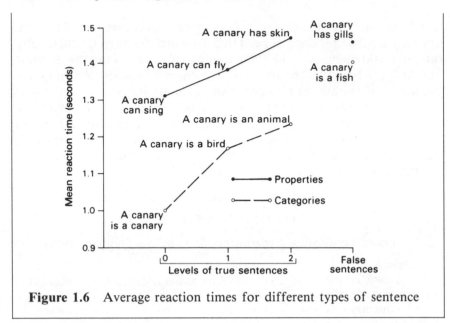

Figure 1.6   Average reaction times for different types of sentence

This study provided general support for the idea that the conceptual categories in a given domain are represented hierarchically. However, subsequent work showed that the model was incorrect in some important details. For one thing, it was found that sentences such as 'a dog is a mammal' took longer to verify than 'a dog is an animal'. Yet according to the hierarchy adopted by Collins and Quillian, the second sentence requires a search through more levels. The most probable reason for this is that 'mammal' is a more unusual category. In a recent study, I asked Ss to draw up their own hierarchies of zoological terms taken from different levels in the scientific taxonomy. Some Ss were uncertain or mistaken about the correct location of terms such as 'mammal' within the animal kingdom, and this was related to how much they knew about zoology. Collins and Quillian's model failed to allow for differences in *knowledge*, which might affect the specific hierarchical structures used by different individuals to represent animal categories. Indeed, the zoological hierarchy which Collins and Quillian adopted in their model was only their own much simplified version of the taxonomy used by zoologists. The importance of individual knowledge in determining how concepts are represented was overlooked for many years after Collins and Quillian proposed their model.

The second finding which casts doubt on the model was that certain pairs of sentences produced differences in verification times even though both involved a search through the same number of levels.

For instance, 'a robin is a bird' might be more rapidly verified than 'a parrot is a bird'. This led psychologists to question whether all the instances within a given category really do have equal status—as would be expected if they are the clearly defined categories which Collins and Quillian imply. What they found was that, in experimental tasks, certain items are judged more typical of a conceptual category than others. Thus subjects in such experiments think of 'robin' as a more typical instance of 'bird' than 'parrot'. This single insight was what most influenced psychologists such as Eleanor Rosch to rethink traditional views of representation.

To conclude, Collins and Quillian's model was innovative in attempting to represent real-life categories, and in showing that individual categories are related to one another within hierarchies. However, like many later models it made simplistic assumptions about these hierarchies. The model was traditional in assuming (at least initially) that individual conceptual categories are represented as lists of properties applying equally to all category members.

Summary of Section 4

● The study of conceptual categorization is concerned with three main questions:
  How are conceptual categories mentally represented?
  By what processes are particular items assigned to these categories?
  By what strategies are these categories acquired?
● Bruner *et al.* (1956) presented items such as simple geometric shapes in experimental studies of the strategies by which people attain concepts specified as conceptual rules. The main classes of strategies used by Ss are *focusing* and *scanning*.
● There has been a gradual shift away from Bruner's approach, towards an emphasis upon how people mentally represent real concepts, rather than how they acquire artificial concepts defined by conceptual rules.
● Collins and Quillian (1969) proposed that concepts of living organisms are represented as a hierarchy of categories, each linked to a list of defining properties. Sentence verification studies supported the general notion of conceptual hierarchies but indicated that individual knowledge of categories, and the varying typicality of category members must be taken into account.

5   How are concepts represented?

Both Bruner and Collins and Quillian assumed that individual concepts are represented by lists of properties or features, and that these properties define the concepts. They are by no means the first to have put forward this view, (which we will henceforth refer to as the *traditional view*). In fact, it originally came from the Greek philosopher Aristotle!

In this section we will consider some of the empirical findings particularly those of Rosch, which have cast doubt on this traditional view of how concepts are represented. It is interesting to consider how far these studies are successful in reflecting fundamental characteristics of cognition rather than the *demand characteristics* of specific experimental tasks.

5.1   Typicality effects

Some of the most persuasive empirical evidence against the traditional view of conceptual structure consists of *typicality effects*. In a whole series of experiments Eleanor Rosch and others have shown that many categories of everyday objects appear to have *internal structure*. That is, the members of a category such as 'furniture' are not thought of as being equal in status. Some members (e.g. chair) are thought of as more typical than others (e.g. wardrobe), thus imparting structure to the category.

TECHNIQUES BOX C

Studies of Typicality Ratings (Rosch 1973, 1975)

Rationale
To investigate whether some members of conceptual categories are thought of as 'better' or more typical examples than others.

Method
Ss were presented with the names of familiar categories, each followed by a randomly ordered list of category members, e.g. Furniture: table, bed, desk, rocking chair, etc. The categories used for the task were: furniture, vehicle, weapon, carpenter's tool, toy, sport, clothing, fruit, vegetable, bird.

For each category, Ss were asked to rate each category member according to how good an example it is of the category. Here is an extract from Rosch's instructions:

> You are to rate how good an example of the category each member is on a 7-point scale. A '1' means that you feel the member is a very good example of your idea of what the category is. A '7'

---

means you feel the member fits very poorly with your idea or image of the category (or is not a member at all). A '4' means you feel the member fits moderately well. For example, one of the members of the category *fruit* is *apple*. If apple fits well with your idea or image of fruit put a 1 after it; if apple fits your idea of fruit very poorly you would put a 7 after it; a 4 would indicate moderate fit. Use the other numbers of the 7-point scale to indicate intermediate judgement.   (Rosch, 1975, p. 198)

Large numbers of Ss were used for such studies in order to provide *normative* data.

Results
1 In Rosch's studies, Ss reported that they found the task simple and that it seemed quite natural to think of category items as differing in how well they exemplify the category.
2 There was a high level of agreement between ratings given by different Ss, i.e. if one S rated a particular item as a good example, other Ss were likely to do the same.
3 Further studies showed that the ratings Ss produce in these tasks are little affected by familiarity or frequency of the category words being rated, i.e. Ss rate 'table' as a good example of furniture because they think of it as typical, *not* because the word 'table' is more familiar than other words such as 'bureau'.

Table 2 on page 46 shows the mean ratings given by Ss for the category 'furniture', ordered from 'best' to 'poorest' examples.

Conclusion
Ss think of some category members as better examples (more typical members) than others.

Activity 3
Below is a list of items taken from the category 'vegetable':

onion	lettuce	broccoli	aubergine
pumpkin	parsnip	pea	rice
leek	kale	parsley	greens

Use the rating scale explained in Techniques Box C to rate each item according to how well you think it exemplifies the category. It does not matter if you give the same rating to more than one item. Once you have given each item a rating, arrange the list of items in order, from the one(s) you have given the highest typicality rating to the one(s) you have given the lowest. Do this *without* referring to Table 3. Now compare your list of ratings with those given in Table 3. Are they similar or different?

Table 2   Norms for goodness-of-example ratings for 'furniture' (from Rosch, 1975, Table A1)

Member	Goodness of example Rank	Specific score	Member	Goodness of example Rank	Specific score
chair	1.5	1.04	lamp	31	2.94
sofa	1.5	1.04	stool	32	3.13
couch	3.5	1.10	hassock	33	3.43
table	3.5	1.10	drawers	34	3.63
easy chair	5	1.33	piano	35	3.64
dresser	6.5	1.37	cushion	36	3.70
rocking chair	6.5	1.37	magazine rack	37	4.14
coffee table	8	1.38	hi-fi	38	4.25
rocker	9	1.42	cupboard	39	4.27
love seat	10	1.44	stereo	40	4.32
chest of drawers	11	1.48	mirror	41	4.39
desk	12	1.54	television	42	4.41
bed	13	1.58	bar	43	4.46
bureau	14	1.59	shelf	44	4.52
davenport	15.5	1.61	rug	45	5.00
end table	15.5	1.61	pillow	46	5.03
divan	17	1.70	wastebasket	47	5.34
night table	18	1.83	radio	48	5.37
chest	19	1.98	sewing machine	49	5.39
cedar chest	20	2.11	stove	50	5.40
vanity	21	2.13	counter	51	5.44
bookcase	22	2.15	clock	52	5.48
lounge	23	2.17	drapes	53	5.67
chaise longue	24	2.26	refrigerator	54	5.70
ottoman	25	2.43	picture	55	5.75
footstool	26	2.45	closet	56	5.95
cabinet	27	2.49	vase	57	6.23
china closet	28	2.59	ashtray	58	6.35
bench	29	2.77	fan	59	6.49
buffet	30	2.89	telephone	60	6.68

SAQ 8
Can you think of any reason why different groups of subjects might produce different ratings? Hint: Rosch's studies were conducted in the USA.

From the findings discussed in Techniques Box C, Rosch concluded that typicality is fundamental to the way people mentally represent conceptual categories. She proposed that members of a category are

Table 3 Norms for goodness-of-example ratings for 'vegetable' (from Rosch, 1975, Table A1)

Member	Goodness of example Rank	Specific score	Member	Goodness of example Rank	Specific score
pea	1	1.07	potato	29	2.89
carrot	2	1.15	parsnip	30	2.91
green beans	3	1.18	turnip greens	31	2.95
string beans	4	1.21	collard	32	2.99
spinach	5	1.22	wax beans	33	3.02
broccoli	6	1.28	watercress	34	3.04
asparagus	7	1.41	blackeyed peas	35	3.06
corn	8	1.55	leek	36	3.15
cauliflower	9	1.62	peppers	37	3.21
brussels sprouts	10	1.72	sweet potato	38	3.27
squash	11	1.83	yams	39	3.31
lettuce	12	1.85	parsley	40	3.32
celery	13	1.90	endive	41	3.39
cucumber	14	2.05	rutabaga	42	3.42
beets	15	2.08	mushroom	43	3.56
greens	16	2.18	avocado	44	3.62
tomato	17	2.23	rhubarb	45	3.66
lima beans	18	2.28	kale	46	3.67
artichokes	19	2.32	escarole	47	3.90
turnip	20	2.37	sauerkraut	48	4.18
aubergine	21	2.38	pickles	49	4.57
romaine	22	2.44	baked beans	50	4.73
green peppers	23.5	2.49	pumpkin	51	4.74
okra	23.5	2.49	seaweed	52	5.04
radishes	25	2.51	garlic	53	5.07
onions	26	2.52	dandelion	54	5.20
bean	27	2.54	peanut	55	5.56
green onion	28	2.60	rice	56	5.59

mentally 'ordered' according to their typicality. Metaphorically, the most typical members are at the 'centre' of the category and the least typical members at the 'edge' with a *dimension of typicality* between the two. But just how fundamental is typicality? It could be argued that while Ss produce typicality ratings in experiments, they do not mentally represent categories in this way. Though Rosch placed emphasis on the fact that her Ss considered the task natural, these introspective reports cannot be counted as strong evidence in her favour. Even the high level of agreement between different Ss' ratings is inconclusive. Perhaps large numbers of Ss were merely tackling the experimental task in the same way.

More persuasive is the fact that typicality affects people's performance in various cognitive tasks. This does suggest that typicality plays a part in the way people organize conceptual knowledge. One such task is *semantic categorization*, described in Techniques Box D. Notice that it is very similar to the sentence verification task described in Techniques Box B.

TECHNIQUES BOX D

The Effects of Typicality on Semantic Categorization (Rosch, 1973)

Rationale
To investigate whether the typicality of a category word affects the time taken to decide if it is a member of a semantic category. If people represent categories in terms of typicality, category judgements should be faster for typical items.

Method
On each trial, the S was given the name of a *target* concept such as 'bird' followed by a *test* item such as 'robin'. The S had to decide as quickly as possible whether or not the test item was a member of the target category. See Table 4 for examples.

Table 4

Trial	Target concept	Test item	Correct response
1	Furniture	Chair	Yes
2	Vegetable	Table	No
3	Furniture	Rug	Yes
4	Vegetable	Carrot	Yes
5	Vegetable	Mushroom	Yes

Results
1 The times for 'yes' responses were affected by typicality—the more typical the test item (as judged in separate studies of typicality ratings) the faster the time taken to decide that it was a member of the target category.
2 Error rates were affected by typicality—there are fewer errors in categorizing more typical words.

SAQ 9
Comparing Table 4 with Tables 2 and 3 work out which of the items in the following pairs should be categorized faster:

    1 or 3?

    4 or 5?

There are many versions of the semantic categorization task all of which show that typicality can affect the *speed* with which category membership is judged. Other studies by Rosch indicate that typicality can affect the order in which category items are remembered or learned. For instance, when Ss are asked to list all the members of a given category they tend to produce items in order of their typicality. Similarly, studies of children suggest that they tend to learn typical members of a category before atypical members. In short, typicality affects people's performance in a wide variety of cognitive tasks.

5.2   Fuzzy boundaries

A second line of empirical evidence against the traditional view of conceptual structure comes from studies of the boundaries of categories. According to the traditional view, these boundaries should be clear-cut and stable. For example, there should be no difficulty in deciding whether a given item of furniture is a chair or a stool, and no change in the way it is categorized depending on context. But, as we saw in Activity 2, these assumptions are questionable. Empirical evidence that the boundaries of certain categories are fuzzy and context-dependent comes from a study by Labov (1973) described in Techniques Box E.

TECHNIQUES BOX E

The Effect of Context on Conceptual Categorization (Labov 1973)

Rationale
To investigate whether people categorize pictures of objects differently depending on the context. If so, this implies that the category boundaries are not clear-cut and unchanging.

Method
In Labov's study, Ss were shown a series of twenty drawings of objects resembling household receptacles, and asked to name the objects depicted. Figure 1.7a shows the first four drawings: the first drawing bears a strong resemblance to a cup, and the remaining drawings are progressively less cup-like.

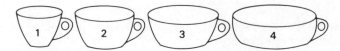

Figure 1.7a The first four drawings used by Labov

Ss performed under one of four context conditions, the context being determined by the instructions given to them for naming the receptacle.

Context condition	Instructions given to Ss
Neutral	Imagine the object held in someone's hand.
Coffee	Imagine someone holding the object and drinking coffee from it.
Food	Imagine the object filled with mashed potatoes and sitting on the dinner table.
Flower	Imagine the object on a shelf filled with cut flowers.

Results
A summary of results is shown in Figure 1.7b.

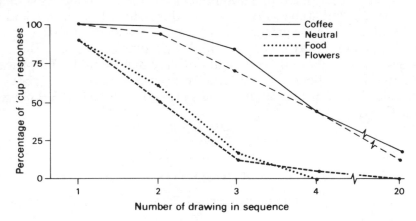

Figure 1.7b The percentage of 'cup' responses for the first four drawings, in four different context conditions

As Figure 1.7b clearly shows, context had an effect on how subjects classified the object. For drawing number one, all Ss in the 'neutral' and 'coffee' conditions, and most Ss in the 'food' and 'flower' conditions gave the response 'cup'. For drawing number two—whose dimensions are slightly less cup-like—all 'neutral' Ss and most 'coffee' Ss continued to give the response 'cup'. However, only approximately 60% of 'food' Ss, and 50% of 'flower' Ss were still calling the receptacle a cup. By the third drawing, the percentage of 'cup' responses for 'food' and 'flowers' subjects were very low indeed—these Ss tended to give the response 'bowl' and 'vase' respectively. Even Ss in the neutral and coffee conditions were no longer consistently calling the object a cup.

Conclusion
The same object (presented as a picture) can be classified differently depending on the context. This implies that Ss defined the boundary of the category 'cup' differently depending on the contextual condition—i.e. the boundary is flexible rather than fixed. Also, there is no abrupt decline in the number of 'cup' responses from one drawing to the next, but a gradual transition from this response to others. Hence the boundary of the category appears to be fuzzy rather than clear-cut.

Again these results cast doubt on the traditional view of category structure. Notice however that the stimulus material in Labov's study consisted of simple drawings. It could be argued that, just as Bruner's artificially constructed stimuli shaped the conclusions drawn from his experiment, so the present materials produce a bias in the way Ss respond. Perhaps *real* cups are more clearly distinguished from other household receptacles.

A more important qualification of Labov's result is that his study only looked at everyday household objects. While the boundaries of such categories may be fuzzy or ill-defined, it does not follow that all categories have ill-defined boundaries. We have already seen that certain categories such as 'triangle' may be well-defined. We also saw that some classes (e.g. living organisms) lend themselves to alternative representations depending on the purposes and knowledge of the individual. One philosopher who definitely rejects the idea that these classes have fuzzy boundaries has commented as follows:

> If a Pekinese is not properly, or only peripherally, a dog, then what other living kind could it be confused with? It may be difficult to decide where 'red' ends and 'orange' starts or where 'cup' leaves off and 'bowl' begins, but it is most certainly not so for 'dog', 'oak' or any other such living kind.   (Atran, 1985)

5.3   Attributes, levels and typicality

One argument against the traditional view is that for years psychologists, philosophers and others have tried to generate defining properties or attributes for conceptual categories such as 'chair', and have failed. Yet some of these people still support the traditional view, maintaining that these properties merely await discovery. In one set of studies, Rosch and her colleague Mervis (1975) sought to tackle this problem afresh by asking experimental Ss to list the attributes they associate with the members of particular categories. Rosch assumed that in generating attribute lists Ss would directly 'externalize' their mental representations for these categories.

The study conducted by Rosch and Mervis is described in Techniques Box F. It is similar to the listing of characteristics which you attempted in the Activities in Section 3.

TECHNIQUES BOX F

Attributes of Category Members (Rosch and Mervis 1975)

Rationale

To investigate what attributes Ss list for members of conceptual categories. The traditional view predicts that Ss should list a common set of attributes for all members of a category, such as 'fruit', there being no overlap with the lists generated for contrast categories, such as 'vegetable'. Rosch and Mervis predicted that Ss should list more shared attributes for typical than for atypical members of a category and that there should be an overlap with the attributes listed for members of contrast categories.

Method

Ss were given randomly ordered lists of terms belonging to particular conceptual categories such as fruit, vegetables, furniture. The terms included ranged from highly typical items such as 'orange' to atypical items such as 'coconut' as rated in Rosch's earlier studies (see Techniques Box C). For each term Ss were asked to list the attributes (such as 'juicy', 'sweet') they associate with it.

Results

On the whole there was agreement across Ss on which attributes they listed for particular category members. For instance, most Ss listed attributes such as 'sweet', 'juicy', 'pips', 'round', for a highly typical fruit such as orange. Ss did not list this same set of attributes for all of the other members of a category. For other typical category members (e.g. grape) Ss tended to list many though not all of the same attributes (e.g. 'sweet', 'juicy', 'pips'). For atypical category members Ss listed few of these shared attributes (e.g. only 'round' and 'sweet' for coconut) plus some of the attributes they list for contrast categories, e.g. Ss listed 'hard' and 'fibrous' for coconut and also for vegetables such as carrot and celery.

These results are as Rosch and Mervis predicted and contrary to the traditional view.

SAQ 10
In a replication of Rosch and Mervis' experiment using British Ss, Ss were asked to list the attributes they associated with types of vegetable, including potato, corn, carrot and peanut. Ss also gave a typicality rating for each vegetable. Most Ss rated potato as the most typical vegetable. Some of the attributes they listed are in the left-hand column of Table 5 below. In the three columns for corn, carrot, peanut, ticks indicate a 'potato' attribute which was also listed for this vegetable. On the basis of the attributes shared with potato, what would you expect to be the order of rated typicality for the three other vegetables?

Table 5

Potato	Corn	Carrot	Peanut
brown			√
round	√		
dirty		√	
eyes			
peel		√	
muddy		√	
vegetable	√	√	

(Based on Conway, 1984)

Rosch and Mervis concluded that since Ss are able to list attributes of category members, attributes (or features) play a role in mentally representing these categories. The role of attributes is not to define the categories by providing all-or-none criteria for membership, but to characterize the categories in terms of what they are most typically like. In this way attributes provide a basis for what Rosch had earlier described as 'internal structure'. The items which Ss rate as typical are those which share many of the attributes commonly associated with the category and few of those associated with contrast categories. The opposite is true of atypical category members.

One way to think of this internal structure is as a *family resemblance*. In a family some members share some features in common (e.g. brown eyes), others share others (e.g. blonde hair). The closer members share more features in common, but no two members of the family (except identical twins) have an identical set of features. In the same way typical category members are those with a high degree of family resemblance, i.e. many attributes in common with other members of the same category; few with members of contrast categories. Atypical members are those with a low degree of family resemblance (few attributes in common with other category members; many with members of contrast categories).

However, Rosch and Mervis's results cannot be regarded as conclusive. It could be argued that Ss do possess defining properties for the conceptual categories investigated but that they do not generate them in this kind of task. Indeed, Ss may have been biased against listing defining properties by the instructions which Rosch and Mervis gave them. For one thing, these instructions did not ask Ss to supply defining characteristics of the categories—rather they asked what attributes Ss *associate* with these categories. Secondly, Rosch's instructions may have encouraged Ss to list *perceptual* features, so it could be that they were biased against listing precisely those attributes (e.g. *functional* ones) which are shared by all category members. All the same, the variation in the attributes listed for different category members is striking and it seems unlikely that a bias in Ss' responses is the only source for this.

Summary of Section 5

In studies designed to question the traditional view of concept representation, it was shown:

- That Ss can rate members of a category such as fruit or furniture according to how well they exemplify the category. Rosch concluded from this that such categories are internally structured according to the typicality of their members.
- That Ss can categorize typical category members more quickly than atypical category members. Rosch concluded that typicality is fundamental to the way these categories are represented.
- That context affects how Ss categorize pictures of everyday household objects. Rosch concluded that the boundaries of these categories are ill-defined or fuzzy.
- That Ss list more shared attributes for typical than atypical category members, and for atypical members there is an overlap with the attributes listed for members of contrast categories. Rosch concluded that such categories are not represented in terms of 'necessary and sufficient' defining properties.

6   Rosch's models of concept representation

The three sets of results quoted in the previous section present a picture of concept representation quite different from that which the traditional view implied. Instead of being clearly specified in terms of defining properties, the concepts investigated seem to be imprecisely represented by the characteristics of typical members. Instead of being clearly distinguished from one another, these concepts appear to have fuzzy boundaries which vary with context. There have been numerous attempts to summarize these findings in the form of models. Rosch herself denies that her interpretations of the results amount to a model, but she has certainly made formal theoretical proposals which for convenience we will refer to as models. Rosch's name is usually associated with the so-called *prototype model*. In practice, because her ideas underwent considerable evolution, it is possible to discern different versions of this model in her work, which we will consider in the ensuing discussion.

Rosch also proposed a model which considers concepts as members of hierarchies. This model is not directly concerned with the part played by typicality in the internal structure of these concepts, but it is an important complement to Rosch's views on this problem. We will consider this model in Section 6.3.

The common goal of all Rosch's theoretical proposals was to suggest concept representations which satisfy the requirements of perceived world structure and cognitive economy discussed in Section 2. For instance, the representation for the concept 'chair' should include just the essential information about how chairs resemble one another and differ from other objects, so that novel instances of this concept can be correctly categorized. The requirement that concepts are shareable between members of a culture (see Section 2.3) is also important, though it was not explicitly stated by Rosch.

6.1   The original prototype model

Rosch's studies led her to conclude that people do not mentally represent categories in terms of defining attributes. Indeed, prior to the attribute listing study described in Techniques Box F, she had proposed that lists of attributes play *no* part in these mental representations. Instead, she suggested that the conceptual representation of a given category is lodged in a *prototype*. She initially saw this as a kind of composite, or amalgamation in abstract form, of the most typical members of the category. She further proposed that between the prototype and the category boundary there is a 'distance dimension' which represents the range of variation from most typical to least typical instance of the category. This is the *typicality dimension*.

It is important to grasp that the prototype of a category was not meant to correspond to any single category member. So the mental prototype for 'chair' was not supposed to be a kitchen chair or any other specific type of chair, though it would be more like a kitchen chair than a garden chair, which is rated as an atypical chair. In some ways Rosch's original prototype is like a mental image. For instance, if you bring to mind your image of a typical chair, you will probably find that it does not correspond to any specific chair or type of chair that you know, but is a composite of these. This captures some of the flavour of a prototype as Rosch first described it. However, Rosch emphasized that prototypes are not necessarily mental images, so this analogy should not be carried too far.

Like the prototype itself, the typicality dimension was supposed to be an abstraction representing the range of variation from the prototype to the category boundary, rather than a series of discrete instances.

Rosch explicitly avoided any proposal about the *processes* by which instances are assigned to particular categories. Yet to be complete such a model should be able to explain how one decides, say, that an item of furniture is a chair and not a table. One suggestion which is frequently associated with the model is that we estimate the overall similarity of a given item to the prototypes of different categories. The item is assigned to the category whose prototype it resembles most. For instance, an odd four-legged object would be compared with the prototypes of categories such as table and chair, and assigned to the one it resembled most. This categorization would be based on overall similarity, rather than any comparison of the individual features of object and prototype.

The model was specifically developed to account for typicality effects, so it has no difficulty in explaining the results described in Section 5.1. People rate category members as good or poor exemplars (Techniques Box C) because they mentally represent categories in terms of an abstraction based on typical members. The processing assumption associated with the model explains why typicality affects the speed of tasks such as semantic categorization (see Techniques Box D). A test item such as 'chair' which closely resembles the prototype for the target category 'furniture' will be more readily categorized than an item such as 'clock' which does not resemble the prototype very much.

The notion that categories have fuzzy boundaries—discussed in Section 5.2—is also in keeping with this early prototype model. The whole point of the model is to suggest that we have an idea of what a typical cup is like (i.e. a prototype), but no clear way of defining a boundary as to what is a cup and what is a bowl. The effect of providing a context—as in the experiment described in Techniques Box E—is presumably to *suggest* a possible categorization (cup, bowl or vase) for the object. Provided the presented object bears some general resemblance to the prototype for this category, it can be included in the category.

The real problem with the early prototype model is the difficulty of specifying exactly what is a prototype—defined as a kind of 'composite' of the most typical members of a category. For instance, according to this definition, the prototype for the category 'fruit' should be a 'mental object' somewhere between an orange, an apple, a banana and other typical fruit. But if we try to imagine what such an item might be like, we come up with a rather weird object, which seems extremely atypical of the category.

In her efforts to clarify the prototype model, Rosch appears to have abandoned the original notion of a prototype as a single composite—a sort of mental 'blob'. At one stage, she even proposed that each conceptual category is represented by the best examples (also called exemplars) of a category that a person has encountered. According to this view, the representation for the category 'fruit' is not a single 'mental object' somewhere between an orange, an apple, a banana and other typical fruit. Instead it is a number of 'mental objects' corresponding individually to an orange, an apple, a banana and other typical fruits that have been encountered.

However, as Rosch was well aware, this idea is not very convincing. A set of specific exemplars will not necessarily include all the relevant shared properties of the category, nor is it economical in cognitive terms. Moreover, since an individual's concepts are assumed to consist of those exemplars he has personally encountered, his concepts could be highly idiosyncratic, sharing little in common with other people's. A representation which summarizes and abstracts what is most typical about the category seems more likely to satisfy the requirements of perceived world structure, cognitive economy and shareability constraints. Rosch therefore made little attempt to elaborate this *exemplar model*, though there have been recent attempts to produce more plausible versions of it (see Smith and Medin, 1981, for discussion).

Rosch's other solution to the difficulty of defining 'prototypes', was to consider whether attributes or features might be involved. As already mentioned, Rosch's original intention in proposing prototypes was to challenge the idea that categories are represented in terms of *defining* features. Yet the difficulty of specifying prototypes in any other way, led her to suggest that attributes or features might serve the purpose: acting not as defining attributes common to all category members but as characteristic attributes which together represent what is most typical and distinctive of the category. This new view—based on the study in Techniques Box F—constitutes a 'feature list' version of her original model. It retains the notion that a prototype is a summary and abstraction constructed from typical members of a category. However, instead of describing this prototype as a kind of composite—a mental 'blob'—it assumes it to be a collection of the features most strongly associated with the concept.

6.2   *Prototypes as feature lists*

This second model obviously shares something in common with models proposed by Bruner and later by Collins and Quillian in assuming that concepts are represented as feature lists. The novel proposal in Rosch's *feature model* is that the feature list for a category typifies rather than defines the category.

According to this model, each of the features which make up the prototype is mentally represented, together with a 'weighting' (termed a *cue validity*) which indicates how distinctively the feature is associated with that concept. For instance, a feature such as 'sweet' is frequently associated with the concept 'fruit', and only rarely associated with the contrast concept 'vegetable'. This feature is said to have a high cue validity for the concept fruit because it would be helpful in deciding whether an item was a fruit or a vegetable. A feature such as 'crunchy' which is sometimes associated with both fruit and vegetables has a lower cue validity for fruit than 'sweet' because it would not be much use in deciding whether an item was a fruit or a vegetable. Rosch computed actual values of cue validities from results of attribute listing tasks like those in Techniques Box F.

Typicality is built into this feature model as follows: typical members of the category are those which possess most of the features that have high cue validity for the category. For instance, 'orange' is a highly typical fruit because it possesses features such as 'juicy', 'sweet', 'pips' etc.—each of which has a high weighting or high cue validity for fruit. 'Coconut' is a less typical fruit because it possesses fewer of these features with high cue validity. The degree to which the features of each fruit overlap with those of other more and less typical fruit is responsible for the family resemblance structure of the whole category (see Section 5.3).

SAQ 11

(a) The following are all features which may be associated with the concept 'bird'. What do you think is the relative cue validity of the three features for the concept? i.e. which feature would be most useful and which least useful in deciding if a 'thing' was a bird?

> Brown colour
> Feathers
> Flies

(b) Which of the following birds possess more of the features with high cue validity, and should therefore be more typical of the concept?

> Parrot
> Emu

Again Rosch does not associate the model with any specific categorization processes, but the following account is consistent with the model. Imagine a person trying to decide whether or not a particular object is an instance of the concept 'chair'. The original prototype model assumed a global comparison of the object with the stored prototype for 'chair' and contrast categories such as 'bench', 'stool', etc. The feature model assumes that the features of the object are compared with the stored feature lists that represent 'chair' and its contrast categories. For each feature of the object which matches a feature in the stored representation for 'chair', the appropriate cue validity is computed from the stored representation. The cue validities of all matched features are added together and if the sum exceeds some threshold value for categorization as a chair, the instance is classified as an instance of this concept.

How does this second model handle the empirical phenomena discussed in Section 5? The fact that Ss rate some category members as more typical than others (see Techniques Box C) can be directly explained on the assumption that the features of these category members add up to a higher weighted feature sum.

The processing assumption outlined above for the model provides a possible explanation for the fact that typicality affects the speed of semantic categorization (see Techniques Box D). The model implies that Ss compare the features of test items such as 'orange' with those of target concepts such as 'fruit' in order to compute weighted feature sums for the test items. Since typical items share more of the highly weighted features associated with the target concept, a weighted feature sum which exceeds the threshold will be achieved more quickly. Similarly, since there are many features in common between test item and target, there will be less chance of an erroneous classification.

The second class of evidence to be considered concerns the boundaries of conceptual categories (Section 5.2). The idea that categories have fuzzy boundaries is implied by the model, since it allows for an overlap between the weighted feature lists which represent different concepts.

The fact that context can affect category boundaries (Techniques Box C) is slightly more taxing for the model. A possible explanation is that the weightings or cue validities attached to particular features can actually be adjusted depending on context. For instance, if the context encourages a person to think that an object is a receptacle for drinking coffee, he may attach little importance to whether it has a handle or not. So he will classify the object as a 'cup' even if it does not have a handle. Effectively he has lowered the cue validity of a handle as a feature which is important in identifying cups. However, this is a somewhat *ad hoc* proposal, and it is not clear how, or under what circumstances, these changes in cue validities might occur.

Finally, the attribute listing task described in Techniques Box F (Section 5.3) needs little explaining because the model is a specific extension of these findings. Features which Ss list frequently for typical members of one concept, and rarely for contrast concepts, are assumed to have high cue-validity. Features which Ss list less frequently for the typical members and sometimes list for contrast concepts are assumed to have lower cue validity. The particular merit of the model is that a concept representation indicates both what the concept is typically like and what it is not.

However, the model poses some important theoretical problems. For one thing, it implies that peoples' knowledge of particular categories is confined to *lists* of their features. But in practice people also know a lot about the *relationship* between features. For instance, our knowledge of chairs includes knowledge of the relationship between the constituent features. Having four legs is a typical feature of tables as well as chairs, but having four legs and a straight back rest is only typical of chairs. Similarly, comparing different types of chairs: soft upholstery tends to go with arms (in armchairs and settees); whereas hard wooden seats tend to go with straight back rests (in kitchen and dining chairs). Indeed, it could be argued that by combining these individual features together into larger 'units', one is identifying *higher order features* which help to characterize a concept.

At the same time, the model fails to specify *components* of features which may help to characterize a concept. That is, it implies that concepts are mentally represented by units of the size which Rosch's Ss listed in her experiments. In practice people may differentiate these 'features' into smaller units which may play a significant role in representation. For instance, wings are a feature of both birds and bats. But as you may be aware, the components of bird wings and bat wings are quite different — a bat wing consists of a web of skin stretched over a bony frame; a bird wing has feathers attached to bones similar in structure to those in the human arm and wrist. Thus the common 'feature' of bats and birds can be broken down into smaller features which differ between the two categories.

To summarize, the model fails to specify both relationships between features and components of features which may play an important part in representing concepts. Despite these difficulties Rosch based her model of conceptual hierarchies discussed in the next section on a feature representation.

Summary of Sections 6.1 and 6.2

● Rosch proposed two alternative models of the internal structure of categories: the original prototype model, and a feature list version. A third alternative—that concepts are represented by specific exemplars—was initially rejected by Rosch, but has re-emerged in more recent work.

● Rosch's original prototype and feature list models may be contrasted as follows:

	Original Prototype	Feature List
Nature of representation	Composite abstraction based on most typical member plus typicality dimension	List of features abstracted from typical instances and weighted according to strength of association with concept
How an instance is categorized	By measuring overall similarity of instance to categories prototypes	By comparing features of instance with feature lists for categories and computing weighted feature lists for the instance
Which empirical findings are explained by model	Typicality ratings Typicality effects, e.g. speed of categorization Context effects	Typicality ratings Typicality effects, e.g. speed of categorization ?Context effects Attribute listing tasks
Theoretical problems	Nature of representation of prototype not clear	Feature lists do not represent relations between features or components of features

6.3   Conceptual hierarchies and the basic level

So far we have suggested that if I bring to mind a concept such as 'orange', I may think of a prototypical orange, or of the features which an orange typically has, or even of some specific oranges I bought yesterday. But my knowledge of oranges also includes the fact that an orange is a fruit, and that there are several different types of oranges — Jaffa, Seville, Navel, etc. How is all this knowledge about oranges mentally organized? Are some aspects of the knowledge more salient and useful than others? Rosch (Rosch *et al.*, 1976) made the following proposals to account for this:

1 People use hierarchies to mentally represent relationships of class inclusion between categories.
2 The categories at each level within a hierarchy are distinguished by the attributes or features associated with them.
3 Within any hierarchy, there is one level at which the categories are both more informative and more economical than at other levels. This level is the *basic level* for cognitive activities.

We have already discussed some evidence that real-life categories are hierarchically organized according to the features which define their members, in Collins and Quillian's study described in Techniques Box B. The original evidence for the basic level came from studies by the anthropologist Berlin (1972) of how plants are classified by cultural groups such as the Tzeltal Indians of Mexico.

Berlin noted that the category names which are used in such cultures tend to correspond to categories at a particular level in the scientific taxonomy of plants. For instance, in the case of trees, the cultures studied by Berlin were more likely to have terms for a 'genus' such as beech or birch than for general superordinate groupings, or for individual species such as silver birch, copper beech. According to Berlin, this is because categories such as 'birch' and 'beech' are naturally distinctive and coherent groupings — the species they include tend to have common patterns of features such as leaf shape, bark colour and so on. The hierarchical level at which these natural groupings occur, and to which category terms correspond, is said to be the basic level.

Essentially Berlin's findings imply that the requirements of cognitive economy and perceived world structure are best satisfied at one particular level in plant hierarchies. Since members of a basic level category of plants share many distinctive attributes in common, the category itself will be an economical summary which is representative of most of its members, and thus an efficient basis for thinking and communicating.

Rosch and her colleagues argued that the principle of a basic level would be a general property of human categorization. In order to test this claim she investigated a much wider range of hierarchies than the botanical ones studied by Berlin, e.g. man-made objects (such as musical instruments, tools, furniture and clothing) and types of food (namely fruit and vegetables). This meant that she needed to define a more general version of Berlin's hypothesis which would apply to these non-botanical categories. She proposed that a level in any hierarchy should be defined as basic if, relative to other levels in the hierarchy, the category members at this level possess many attributes in common with each other and few in common with contrast categories. These proposals modify but do not contradict Rosch's earlier claim that categories are ill-defined with fuzzy boundaries. What she is saying is that there is one level (the basic level) at which categories are less fuzzy and ill-defined than at the other levels.

Figure 1.8 illustrates two of the three-level hierarchies investigated by Rosch. One is a biological taxonomy of birds, though missing many of the levels which ornithologists use in classifying birds. The other is a hierarchy of everyday objects, namely furniture.

Altogether Rosch investigated three biological hierarchies (tree, fish and bird) and based her predictions as to where the basic level would

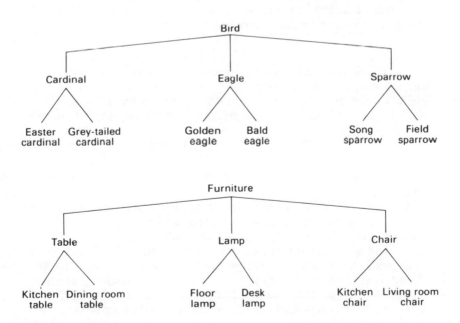

Figure 1.8   Rosch's hierarchies for birds and for furniture (Note: Birds shown are native to North America rather than Great Britain.)

lie on Berlin's findings. For the remaining hierarchies (fruit, vegetables, furniture, musical instruments, tools, clothing, vehicles), Rosch's predictions were based on intuition. (In Rosch's study, 'fruit' and 'vegetable' were not classed as biological categories because in everyday use they distinguish types of food rather than groupings based on scientific criteria.)

SAQ 12
According to Berlin's findings, which level should be basic for the bird hierarchy shown in Figure 1.8? Which level would you intuitively predict to be basic for the furniture hierarchy?

Rosch's investigations of the basic level are discussed in Techniques Box G.

TECHNIQUES BOX G

Attribute Listings for Basic Level Categories (Rosch *et al.* 1976)

Rationale
To investigate the attributes which people list for categories at three different levels in conceptual hierarchies. One level (the intermediate level) is predicted to be the most inclusive level at which Ss lists many attributes common to most category members.

Method
As in Techniques Box F, Ss were presented with lists of category terms and asked to list the attributes they associate with each. For a given hierarchy the presented terms include the superordinate (e.g. fruit), intermediate terms (orange, apple, etc.) and subordinates (Navel orange, Seville orange, etc.)

Results
Table 6 shows a sample of results for the 'furniture' and 'bird' hierarchies.

As predicted, at one level in the 'furniture' hierarchy Ss listed a relatively large number of terms which they also listed for categories at the level below. Thus whereas Ss listed no attributes for 'furniture', they listed eight attributes for 'chair' and also listed these for 'living room chair' and 'kitchen chair'. Only three additional attributes are listed for 'living room chair', and none for 'kitchen chair'. A similar pattern of results occurred for the other non-biological categories, though 'furniture' was the only superordinate for which Ss listed no attributes at all.

For the 'bird' hierarchy it was the superordinate category for which Ss listed numerous distinctive attributes. This pattern of results was common to the three biological hierarchies.

Table 6

Level	Non-biological		Biological	
	Category	Attributes listed	Category	Attributes listed
Super-ordinate	Furni-ture	None	Bird	Feathers Head Wings Claws Beak Lays Legs eggs Feet Nests Eyes Flies Tail Chirps Eats flies and worms

Intermediate (predicted basic level)	Chair	Legs
		Seat
		Back
		Arms
		Comfortable
		Four legs
		Wood
		Holds people—
		    you sit on it
			Sparrow	As for 'Bird'
				    Small
				    Brown

Subordinate	Living room chair	As for 'Chair' plus:
		    Large
		    Soft
		    Cushion
			Song sparrow	As for 'Sparrow'

	Kitchen chair	As for 'Chair'	Field sparrow	As for 'Sparrow'

Rosch concluded that a basic level existed for both the biological and non-biological hierarchies. But her prediction that the intermediate level would be basic was only confirmed for the non-biological hierarchies. It is clear that for the biological hierarchies Rosch's Ss treated the superordinate level categories as basic.

This difference between Rosch's and Berlin's findings for the biological hierarchies is important because it implies that the location of the basic level may vary between individuals or between groups depending on their culture and knowledge. For the average Westerner, the distinctive groupings are at the level of 'tree', 'bird', 'fish', etc. Other cultural groups with more sophisticated knowledge of these hierarchies treat more specific subcategories as distinctive. So-called primitive groups and ornithologists both count as experts on this criterion.

Rosch *et al.* made further studies of the properties of the basic level. For instance, they found that the basic level is the highest one in a hierarchy at which category members are judged to look alike. Thus, members of the category 'chair' are judged to look alike, whereas members of the category 'furniture' are not. This may mean that the basic level is the highest level at which people can form a generalized image of the category.

Rosch *et al.* also claimed that the basic level is the most inclusive level at which people associate similar movements with category members. For instance, the same sitting movement is associated with many different kinds of chairs. There is no common movement associated with different types of furniture.

The general implication of these findings is that one level within conceptual hierarchies—the basic level—is the most convenient for cognitive activities such as memory, perception, communication. Compared with other levels in hierarchies, basic level categories are both informative and economical. For instance, if we mention a basic level term such as 'apple' this conveys much more information than if we mention 'fruit'. If we mention the term 'Cox's apple', this may give more information than is really required.

You may be wondering how Rosch's model of the basic level relates to the two versions of the prototype model discussed earlier. Both these latter models were stimulated by the empirical evidence that conceptual categories are ill-defined and fuzzy. The notion of a basic level represents an important qualification to this general approach. Basic level categories are, by definition, less ill-defined and fuzzy than the others, and this is why they are the 'preferred' categories for cognitive activities.

Throughout our discussion the category 'chair' has been given as an example of an everyday category which is somewhat difficult to define and somewhat difficult to distinguish from contrast categories such as seat, stool, etc. But, as you probably realised, this basic level category has a number of properties which are highly characteristic if not definitive—there are very few chairs which are for more than one person to sit on. Activity 2 in Section 3 would have been even more difficult if the category to be described had been 'furniture', which is a very diffuse, ill-defined category, or 'dining chair', which shares so much in common with 'kitchen chair', etc. This is why Rosch argued that a comprehensive approach to how concepts are represented should consider both the internal structure of individual categories and how they function within hierarchies.

Rosch's original idea of a prototype makes more sense for basic level categories. For instance, it is quite easy to imagine a 'composite abstraction' based on members of the category 'orange' since it will take the form of an image of a typical orange. The difficulty arises if you try to imagine a prototype for the superordinate category 'fruit', since this should be a cross between an orange, an apple, a banana and other typical fruit.

Rosch's concept of cue validity also has a special relevance for basic level categories. A basic level category should have higher total cue validity than categories at other levels because it possesses many features which are strongly associated (apply to many members) and few features which are weakly associated (apply to members of contrast categories).

To conclude, Rosch's account of how concepts are represented comprises quite a complex body of ideas. In order to clarify how these ideas relate to one another, I have drawn up Figure 1.9, which you may like to study. The principle ideas illustrated are as follows:

Hierarchical relationships
The diagram shows the three levels proposed by Rosch, plus a higher superordinate 'food' which subsumes both 'fruit' and 'vegetables'.

Basic level categories
Orange, apple, banana, etc.

Typicality
Fruits range from typical ones such as 'orange' to atypical ones such as 'coconut'; oranges range from typical ones such as 'Jaffa' to atypical ones such as 'Blood orange'.

Prototype representations
Possible for basic level categories and below; difficult for superordinates.

Feature representations
  (i) Features strongly associated with concept and weakly associated with other concepts have high cue validity.
 (ii) Typical category members have more of the features with high cue validity.
(iii) Basic level categories have higher total cue validity.

Exemplar representations
Orange, apple, banana, etc., are all typical exemplars of the category 'fruit'.

Fuzzy boundaries
Features which appear in more than one category lead to category overlap or fuzzy boundaries. Basic level categories have the least fuzzy boundaries. Subordinate categories have very fuzzy boundaries.

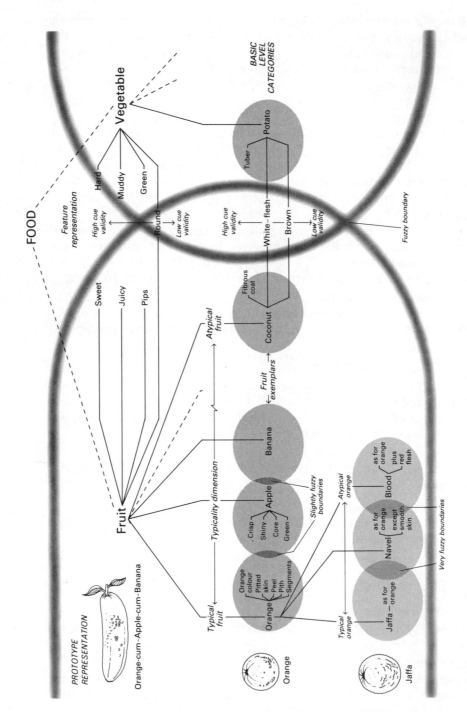

Figure 1.9   A schematic summary of Rosch's models

Summary of Section 6.3

- Rosch proposed that within any conceptual hierarchy there is one level at which the categories are both more informative and more economical than at other levels. This level is the basic level for cognitive activities.
- The basic level is defined as the highest within a hierarchy at which categories have many attributes in common and few in common with contrast categories.
- The basic level reflects those aspects of perceived world structure which are most obviously distinctive for a given culture or expert group.
- The idea of a basic level represents an important qualification to Rosch's fuzzy concept approach.

7   Representing concepts: one model or many?

The main theme for this Part has been how the study of everyday concepts has changed people's theories of conceptual representation. The traditional view which implied that all concepts are represented as clear-cut, well-defined categories was challenged by more recent evidence that some at least are represented as ill-defined, fuzzy categories characterized by what is most typical of them. In Sections 6.1 and 6.2 we considered two alternative models based on these conclusions. But should we regard Rosch's 'fuzzy concept' approach as a straightforward substitute for the traditional view? Rosch's own studies showed that basic level concepts such as 'chair' are less fuzzy and ill-defined than their subordinates such as 'kitchen chair' and 'dining chair', which are hard to distinguish from one another. So even within the general framework of 'fuzzy concepts', not all conceptual categories are represented in an equally fuzzy way.

In this section, we will consider whether Rosch's fuzzy concept approach can be reconciled with elements of the traditional view. One line of argument which has been proposed is that the two modes of representation are appropriate for different types of concept. An alternative view is that both modes of representation can be used for any type of concept, depending on the purposes of the representation and the knowledge of the individual.

7.1   Different representations for different concepts?

Some classes of entities such as the geometric figures discussed in Section 3 do seem to be well-defined 'in themselves'. That is, there are widely agreed rules or descriptions which appear to define these classes. As a first approximation it seems plausible to suggest that a person's mental representations for such classes are correspondingly well-defined and clear-cut. According to this view the traditional model of representation is applicable to specific conceptual domains such as geometric figures.

Rosch set out to study everyday conceptual classes which do not seem well-defined in themselves. Apparently, there are no widely agreed rules for defining different types of tool or furniture. So it is not too surprising that Rosch found people's mental representations for these classes to be correspondingly fuzzy.

It might then be concluded that there are two intrinsically different types of conceptual domain: those such as geometric figures which obviously lend themselves to well-defined representation; and those such as man-made objects which obviously lend themselves to fuzzy representations! If so, an understanding of how concepts are represented should be a simple matter of deciding whether the class of entities under consideration is obviously well-defined or obviously 'fuzzy'. In practice it is by no means simple to divide up the world in this way. On an intuitive basis, everyday categories of man-made objects such as vehicles, tools, furniture, are the obviously fuzzy ones. But on closer scrutiny the notion of an everyday concept is clearly hard to define! For instance, Atran (1985) has argued that biological categories such as animal and plants are intrinsically well-defined, whereas categories of man-made objects are intrinsically fuzzy. In contrast, Rosch assumed that biological categories such as 'dog' and man-made categories such as 'furniture' are both 'everyday' categories which lend themselves to fuzzy representations. In fact, as Table 7 shows, the categories she investigated were a heterogeneous mixture of biological, man-made and other categories, with no clear unifying principle. Indeed, the categories vary on at least four important dimensions. They can be natural, man-made or, in the case of specially bred varieties of fruit and vegetables, somewhere between the two. They can be part of our everyday life or, in the case of weapons, relatively unusual. Most of the categories appear to lack a formal definition, but at least one—bird—can be formally defined. Finally, the categories span both objects and events. Rosch could legitimately have studied abstract concepts such as 'marriage' and 'divorce' too— since they crop up frequently in everyday life. Yet abstract concepts have usually been ruled out of such studies precisely because they do

Table 7

Category	Comments
Furniture Vehicle Carpenter's tool Toy Clothing	Man-made objects in everyday use
Weapon	Man-made objects, but not in everyday use for most people.
Sport	Everyday activities rather than objects. Each sport has its own set of formal rules.
Bird	Everyday objects but natural rather than man-made. Correspond to a taxonomic category which can be scientifically defined.
Fruit Vegetable	Everyday objects. Natural, though man has affected natural types by breeding special varieties! Categories are botanically heterogenous.

not conform to one's intuitive idea of an everyday concept. The point is that since there is no clear way of defining what is meant by an 'everyday' concept, we cannot easily predict which categories will lend themselves to well-defined or fuzzy representations.

To complicate matters, there is both anecdotal and experimental evidence that any concept (whether everyday or unusual, natural or man-made, concrete or abstract) may be represented in different ways, depending on an individual's knowledge, and the purposes of the representation.

7.2   Different representations for the same concept?

A chemist may define substances such as lead, copper, gold, etc. in terms of the numbers of electrons, protons and neutrons in their atoms, whereas people with no expertise in the subject may have much less precise concepts of these substances. *Expert knowledge* is undoubtedly an important dimension in determining how different people represent the same domain. Sometimes it is the layman who divides the world into clear-cut categories, while the expert with greater knowledge, may treat category distinctions as fuzzy. For instance, we divide up the world into living things and non-living things, whereas scientists are aware that particles such as viruses do not fall clearly into either category. A similar point applies to concept pairs such as 'life' and 'death', 'male' and 'female'. We behave as if there were clear-cut boundaries between these categories, yet the definitions of these boundaries are the subject of much debate in medical and legal circles. In one study of how expert knowledge affects categorization, Murphy and Wright (1984) compared concepts of various psychiatric disorders held by experts and novices. They reported that the experts' concepts were actually less distinctive and clear-cut, and concluded that greater knowledge may have led the experts to focus on the *shared* rather than the distinctive features of the disorders.

Not only may different people represent the same concept in different ways, but as I suggested in Section 3 the same individual may hold a *dual representation* of the same concept — a 'fuzzy' one for everyday purposes, and a precise definition which can be called for when precision is required. An elegant illustration of this proposal is provided by Armstrong *et al.* (1983). Take the concept 'grandmother'. Instances of this concept tend typically to share perceptual and functional features, such as grey hair, wrinkles and a twinkle in the eye. Not all members of the class will have these features, and some may have more of them than others. This is precisely what Rosch's studies of attribute listings imply. However, while Rosch concluded that a person's only representation for the concept 'grandmother' would be a list of these typical attributes, it could be argued that this list is merely a superficial representation used to make quick judgements of things, scenes and events in the world. On this view, people also possess a more precise representation of the category, sometimes known as a *conceptual core*. For 'grandmother' this conceptual core will be 'mother of a parent'. In other words, it is a definition which determines membership in an all-or-none fashion.

There may even be several different degrees of precision in representing concepts. For instance, the concept 'gold' may be represented in the following three ways:

1 Yellow glittery stuff
2 Precious yellow non-rusting malleable ductile metal
3 Atomic number 79

The first representation serves for everyday purposes in that it serves to distinguish gold from non-gold on a rough-and-ready basis. The second representation has the degree of precision which a layman might use when precision is called for — though it may not distinguish gold from non-gold on absolutely all occasions. The third representation (which indicates the atomic weight of gold) is a 'factual scientific description' — sometimes termed a *real essence*. The third representation comes closest to the traditional notion of a necessary and sufficient property which applies to all gold and only to gold, though according to contemporary scientific thought even these most clear-cut 'definitions' are potentially fallible.

Given this evidence for several representations of a single concept, it could be argued that Rosch was merely 'scratching at the surface' in her account of how everyday categories are represented. That is, while empirical phenomena such as the typicality effects described in Section 5.1 are *genuine*, they do not rule out the possibility that a person also holds 'core' representations of the categories, which are relatively clear-cut, and well-defined.

In defence of Rosch, it can be argued that not *all* concepts will be represented by *all* people in two, let alone three ways. For instance, as Armstrong *et al.* point out, 'few other than vintners and certain biologists may have much in the way of a serious description of "grape" mentally represented' i.e. in these cases, the fuzzy representation may serve as the only representation of the concept. And where dual representations do occur, this does not deny that a fuzzy description is one of them. It merely challenges Rosch's claim that everyday items are represented *solely* as fuzzy concepts.

7.3 *Fuzzy representations for well-defined concepts?*

The original basis for Rosch's 'fuzzy concept' approach lies in the principle of perceived world structure outlined in Section 2.1. According to this principle certain clusters of properties in the real world are highly correlated. For instance, inanimate objects with four legs *usually* have a flat, supported, surface for putting things on or sitting on. But sometimes four legs is a feature associated with a television or an artist's easel, etc. According to Rosch this state of affairs is represented in categories which have an internal typicality structure. Clusters of properties which are highly correlated in the real world are represented as typical of the category, whereas properties which only occasionally go together are represented as atypical. Notice, however, that some real world correlations are 100%. Thus it is *not* the case that triangles *usually* have three straight sides and angles adding to 180°. They always do! In order to reflect this second state of affairs, the mental representation for triangles should consist of an all-or-none conceptual rule, not a description which applies more to some triangles than others. Thus it is a corollary of Rosch's approach that none of the typicality effects which occur for fuzzy domains should occur for these obviously well-defined domains. The experiments by which Armstrong *et al.* (1983) tested this prediction are described in Techniques Box H.

TECHNIQUES BOX H

Typicality Effects with Well-defined Concepts (Armstrong *et al.* 1983)

Rationale
To investigate whether typicality effects occur for 'well-defined' categories as well as 'everyday' categories. Rosch's theory predicts that typicality effects should occur for 'everyday' concepts but not for 'well-defined' concepts. The dual representation theory predicts that typicality effects will occur for both types of concept.

Method
Experiment 1   Ss were run on a replication of Rosch's (1973, 1975) typicality rating experiments (cf. Techniques Box C). Categories employed were one of two types:

Everyday	*Well-defined*
Sport	Odd number
Vehicle	Even number
Fruit	Female
Vegetable	Geometric figure

Experiment 2   Using the same materials, Ss were run on a replication of a sentence verification task (cf. Techniques Box B). Ss had to verify sentences such as 'An orange is a fruit' in which instances were either good or poor exemplars of their categories as rated in Experiment 1.
Experiment 3   A new set of Ss were asked outright whether membership of the categories (fruit, odd numbers, etc.) is a matter of degree. They were then re-run on Experiment 1.

Results
Experiment 1   Ss produced typicality ratings for items from both everyday and well-defined categories. It apparently made sense to judge certain odd numbers or geometric figures as good examples of their category, e.g. 3 was rated as a better example of an odd number than 23.
Experiment 2   Typicality effects occurred for both everyday and well-defined categories, i.e. Ss verified statements about odd numbers faster, if the items in the statement had been judged typical.
Experiment 3   When a new set of Ss were asked outright if membership of well-defined categories is a matter of degree, they denied it. Yet they still produced typicality ratings when tested on Experiment 1.

The somewhat surprising implication of these findings is that Ss have 'fuzzy' representations constructed from the properties of typical members, even for categories such as odd numbers or geometric figures which seem obviously well-defined. For instance, since Ss judge 'square' to be a good example of a geometric figure, whereas 'ellipse' is judged to be a poor example, this implies that they possess a representation for the category 'geometric figure' which is much more like a square than an ellipse. However, these same Ss are clearly aware that membership of the category 'geometric figure' is not, logically, a matter of degree—a figure either is or is not a member of this category. So presumably Ss possess dual representations even for these obviously well-defined categories.

What is surprising about these results is that at first glance it does not seem cognitively economical to have dual representations, one of which so obviously violates the principle of perceived world structure. If we are well aware that membership of the category 'odd numbers' is not, in reality, a matter of degree, why do we think of the category in this way? A plausible explanation emerges if we think of the general function of fuzzy representations as providing a basis for rapid everyday judgements. If you are asked to explain what a geometric figure is, for many purposes it may be quite sufficient to think of the properties which typical figures such as squares and triangles have. It would probably take much longer to work out the mathematical definition which applies to all geometric figures, and it might be less readily understood by the layman. On the other hand if you were having a conversation with a philosopher or mathematician, it would certainly be advisable to have your core definition of a geometric figure to the fore! In conclusion, though a dual representation may be less economical in terms of memory storage, it may be more economical to have alternative representations which are specifically tailored for different types of thinking and which can be readily shared by different social groups.

Despite the obvious attractions of the dual representation approach, it does pose certain problems. For as Armstrong *et al.* point out, it duplicates at two levels the problems of specifying what the distinctive features of categories are. At the level of the 'fuzzy' representation, the problem is to know which of the supposedly typical features of a category serve as a basis for rough-and-ready identification. At the level of the conceptual core, the problem of specifying features is identical with that of the traditional approach—defining features for most categories are hard to find. Armstrong *et al.* give an interesting account of these problems which you might like to follow up.

Summary of Section 7

- Different models of representation may be necessary depending on the type of concept, individual knowledge, and the purposes of the representation.
- Some types of conceptual category (e.g. geometric figures) seem obviously well-defined, whereas others (e.g. man-made objects) seem obviously fuzzy. However, many categories (e.g. biological ones) are difficult to classify in this way.
- According to the dual representation model, many concepts including well-defined ones lend themselves to two alternative representations — a 'fuzzy' representation which serves as a basis for quick rough-and-ready judgements, and a conceptual core which is used if precise definition is called for.
- Dual representations tailored for different purposes are less economical in terms of memory storage, but may be more economical for thinking and communicating and more readily shared by a particular social group.

8 Conclusion: the importance of expert knowledge

Throughout our discussion one point has kept cropping up: that the way people represent conceptual categories is affected by what they know. This seems an intuitively obvious point, and yet it has been virtually overlooked in the models which have been proposed. An obvious exception from outside psychology is the large body of anthropological work on the categories used by different cultural groups. In many cases cross-cultural differences relate to differences in knowledge and differences in the purposes of classifications. An apparently primitive group such as Eskimos are experts when it comes to distinguishing different types of snow, and this is reflected in the numerous categories they use for snow.

Within cognitive psychology, our understanding of how specialist knowledge affects categorization is incomplete. We have outlined two major modes of representation: well-defined and fuzzy. While it is clear that knowledge affects how people operate these two modes, more research is required to elucidate this issue. For instance, we have suggested that experts operate with concepts which are well-defined compared to the fuzzy concepts used by novices. Yet in some cases it may be the other way round. For instance, experts in medical science may use fuzzy prototypes for rapid identification of abnormal cells, whereas novices working in the same field may need to go more slowly using precise definitions of these cells.

Knowledge may affect which type of fuzzy representation is employed. For instance, children learning a new concept may represent their knowledge about a set of items in terms of a prototype, whereas adults may employ a feature list.

Knowledge may also affect which features appear in such a list. For instance, the layman may treat 'feathers' as a typical feature of birds, and use them in his representation of bird. In contrast, a zoologist may treat 'feathers' as a global structure which can be broken down into component features of a more scientific nature.

Finally, knowledge may affect how people represent relationships between concepts. Though both layman and expert may use conceptual hierarchies for this purpose, the layman may use an intuitive hierarchy quite unlike the taxonomic hierarchies used by experts; both may use a basic level for maximum cognitive economy, but the location of this level may shift with knowledge. Thus, whereas the layman may treat 'birds' as a distinctive grouping, the ornithologist may think in terms of species such as robin and blackbird. All these effects of knowledge require further research.

Further reading

1 Johnson-Laird and Wason (eds) (1977) *Thinking: Readings in Cognitive Science*. Contains a good selection of articles on conceptual thinking and also some on the relationship between language, culture and thought. See particularly article 11 by Sokal, on the general principles of scientific classification.

2 Greene (1986) *Language: A Cognitive Approach*. Contains a discussion of the relationship between concepts and language.

3 Smith and Medin (1981) *Categories and Concepts*. A detailed review of theory and evidence on conceptual categorization.

4 Mervis and Rosch (1981) 'Categorization of natural objects'. An overview of Rosch's approach and its problems.

5 Armstrong, Gleitman and Gleitman (1983) 'What some concepts might not be'. A critique of Rosch and of the dual representation theory.

Part II
An Introduction to Object Perception

Ilona Roth

Part II   Object Perception

Contents

1 *What is perception?*

The term *perception* refers to the means by which information acquired from the environment via the sense organs is transformed into experiences of objects, events, sounds, tastes, etc. In the rest of this volume, we shall focus on the question of how *objects* are perceived, and we shall be dealing exclusively with the *visual modality*. There are of course several other modalities, including hearing, taste, smell, touch and the *kinaesthetic modality* which gives a person information about his or her own movement, bodily position and orientation in space. It is important to remember that although these modalities are usually studied separately, perception frequently integrates information from several modalities at once.

In Part I we discussed how an object with properties such as four legs and straight back tends to be thought of or categorized as a chair. If presented with a real object conforming to this description we actually *perceive* it as a chair. That is, we *recognize* it as a member of the category 'chair'. We may even *identify* the object as a specific chair (e.g. the chair I work on, my daughter's high chair) or as a type of chair (a Chippendale chair, a rocking chair). Object perception then is one of the major ways in which we categorize things, thus dividing the world into meaningful chunks and providing a basis for *action*. Once we have perceived something as a chair, we know what to call it, and what to do with it.

However, object perception has other consequences besides categorization. For instance, besides recognizing an object as a chair, I can perceive what colour it is, how far away it is, whether it is moving (rocking chairs do!). Sometimes an object may be perceived without being assigned to a meaningful category (see Figure 2.1).

Figure 2.1 (Source: Carelman, 1971)

The item pictured in Figure 2.1 is seen as a structured coherent object—perhaps even as a chair-like object—but not as a chair. We can perceive individual parts of the object such as arms, legs, etc., and with some effort we can perceive each of these parts as itself made up of lines, angles and surfaces. In short, *object perception* implies a range of activities, not all of which are concerned with assigning objects to categories. Some people use the term *seeing* for the more basic tasks of perceiving objects as distinct from backgrounds, and reserve the term *object recognition* for any perceptual activity which results in an object being placed in a meaningful category.

The processes by which we see and recognize objects such as chairs seem so subtle that many people are surprised that there is anything to explain. But by considering examples in which perception lacks this seemingly effortless, immediate quality, we can demonstrate that it consists of complex activities which require a certain amount of time.

Try to work out what the picture in Figure 2.2 consists of. Notice that once you have done so it is difficult to dispel the interpretation—it becomes comparatively effortless and immediate. Yet the initial achievement of recognizing the object certainly required time and effort.

Figure 2.2   If you cannot identify this image, turn to page 86 for the answer. (Photo: R. C. James)

In the rest of this volume we will discuss both experimental and computer studies which have helped to elucidate the complex processes and representations underlying perception.

Summary of Section 1

● Perception refers to the means by which the information a person acquires from the environment is transformed into experiences of objects, events, sounds, tastes, etc.

- The perception of objects usually involves recognizing them as members of categories which make sense and which provide a basis for action.
- Object perception also provides other types of information such as the colour and position of an object, whether it is moving, and the parts or features which make it up.
- Object perception frequently seems to be effortless and immediate. However, the underlying processes are complex and take a measurable amount of time.

2   *The image processing framework*

As you have probably realized, object perception is a complex series of sensory and cognitive activities, not all of which can be discussed in this volume. Those aspects which have been selected for discussion mostly fit into the same information processing framework, according to which the *image* formed by light on the retina at the back of the eye is transformed into perception of objects etc. Though this view, often known as *image processing*, is pervasive, it has been rejected by some theorists, such as J. J. Gibson, and his theory will be briefly considered at a later stage. The theories which fall within the image processing framework span several distinct *levels of explanation* which we will now consider.

2.1   *Levels of explanation*

Suppose that you were asked to explain how a complex piece of machinery such as a washing machine works, to someone who had never encountered such a device. How would you set about it? You would probably start by giving a clear description of what the device is for — what *function* it fulfils. So you would explain that if you put dirty clothes into the machine, it washes, rinses and spins them, providing clean clothes which can be hung out to dry. Having stated this general function, you would go on to explain how it is achieved, i.e. how the device *works*. To do this, you would need to describe the main *operating principles* of the washing machine: for instance, pumping water in and out, adding powder, rotating the clothes, maintaining the appropriate water temperature and so on. Next, if your listener was mechanically minded you might find yourself trying to explain the actual *mechanisms* underlying these operating principles!

For instance, you might need to give mechanical details of the thermostat or motor. So to give a complete explanation of the washing machine you might draw on three different levels of explanation.

The late David Marr has argued (1982) that three similarly distinct levels of explanation are required in order to understand visual perception. To start with, it is necessary to give a clear picture of what perception is for, i.e. what are its functions. In addition, one needs to understand how these functions are achieved, i.e. what are the main operating principles of visual perception. Finally, if possible, one should have an understanding of the mechanisms underlying these operating principles, i.e. the *physiology* of visual perception.

According to Marr, the first level, which he terms the *computational theory level*, has priority. Just as one cannot make proper sense of operating principles, such as pumping water or adding detergent, unless one knows what a washing machine is for, so one cannot fully understand perceptual operating principles unless one understands the overall function which they achieve. The overall function of the washing machine is specified by what it starts with (dirty clothes) and what it achieves (clean clothes ready to hang out on the line). Similarly, argues Marr, the function of visual perception is specified by what it starts with—the *input*—and what it achieves—the *output*. In the case of human vision the input is a pattern of light produced by objects and events in the environment which form images on the retina. The output is information about objects and events in the environment which one needs in order to organize action.

Marr uses the term *computation* to refer to the overall strategy by which a visual system achieves its function of transforming inputs into appropriate perceptual outputs. Marr believes that it is only when one has a clear grasp of this computation (a *computational theory*) that one should attempt to specify the underlying operating principles or *algorithms*. These consist of the *processes* and *representations* responsible for converting the input in the form of a visual image, into an output in the form of perceptions of objects, events, etc.

Finally, it is desirable to understand the functioning of the *hardware* which carries out these operating principles. For human vision this hardware corresponds to the neuronal mechanisms of the visual system. Again Marr argues that a proper computational theory is crucial for this understanding. Just as the mechanical workings of a washing machine make more sense if we know what the machine is for, so the hardware of a visual system makes better sense if we understand the overall functions the system achieves. Without the computational theory the visual hardware may be as puzzling as the nuts and bolts of a machine whose function is unknown.

Marr's three levels for understanding human perception are also seen as the levels of analysis which must be used in designing a computer to 'see' objects or scenes. The three levels needed to 'explain' a washing machine would be equally necessary in specifying how to *make* a washing machine. Similarly, in order to design a computer to carry out visual tasks one would need to specify each of the three levels of explanation we have outlined. The first two levels would specify how to program the computer, and the third level would specify how to actually build it. A fuller account of Marr's attempt to design a *vision system* is given in Part III of this volume.

The value of Marr's approach is to show the additional insights into visual perception which can be achieved by integrating the 'computational theory' with an analysis of operating principles and hardware. Historically, however, the main emphasis has been on studies of operating principles and the neuronal mechanisms underlying them. The present Part will therefore give an overview of these findings as a background for Marr's later work.

Summary of Section 2.1

● Three levels of analysis are necessary in order to understand visual perception or to design a computer to carry out visual tasks.

	Levels of analysis	*General specification*	*Marr's terminology*
1	What functions must perception achieve?	To transform inputs in the form of images into outputs in the form of descriptions of objects, events, etc., which provide a basis for action	Computational theory
2	What are the operating principles which achieve these functions?	Processes and representations	Algorithms
3	What are the mechanisms underlying these operating principles?	Neuronal mechanisms of human vision or electronic components of computer	Hardware

2.2   *Processes and representations*

In order to see an object such as a chair at the other side of the room, light reflected from this object must reach the eyes which are the *sense organs* for vision. The light forms an image on the *retina*—the layer of light-sensitive nerve cells at the back of the eye. This is rather like the way that an image is formed on the photo-sensitive film in a camera. However, unlike the film in a camera, the retinal image cannot be removed and developed! Nor can it be directly 'seen' for what it is. It is not a copy of an object, but a *two-dimensional* array of points at which light has stimulated light-sensitive cells. This pattern of points is not even stable since it changes with the slightest movement of the object, or the observer's eyes.

Despite fluctuations in the size and shape of the retinal image produced by a single object, the perception is usually of a stable object whose size and shape does not change. This phenomenon is known as *constancy*. The lack of direct correspondence between fluctuating two-dimensional retinal images and the stable objects which we see and recognize implies that complex *processes* are required to transform one into the other.

In order to recognize an object such as a chair from the information contained in the retinal image, we also need some knowledge about chairs. For instance, the object on the left in Figure 2.3 is not perceived as a proper chair, even though it has many of the same features as the object on the right, which we would recognize as a chair. This is because only the right-hand object fits the conceptual knowledge about chairs which is stored or represented in our memories.

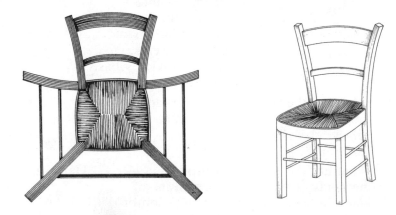

Figure 2.3   (Source: Carelman, 1971)

Figure 2.2 shows a Dalmatian dog sniffing among fallen leaves.

Mental representations, then, are also involved in object perception. However, there are many different views about the nature of these stored representations and the precise role they play in processing inputs. For instance, one class of theories assumes a sequences of stages commencing with a *low-level analysis* of the retinal image, and building up gradually to an 'interpretation' based on a comparison with stored knowledge. This idea is termed *bottom-up processing* to denote a processing sequence which starts at the input and builds upwards to an interpretation. According to this bottom-up approach, stored knowledge about the properties of objects, scenes etc. plays no role in processing the input, until the final stage at which an 'interpretation' is made. Suppose that we know that four vertical legs and a horizontal seat are typical features of chairs; we will use this information, not to guide our analysis of retinal input, but only to draw the final conclusion that the object we see is a chair. This mode of processing information is also known as *data-driven processing* because it is guided or driven solely by the sensory data which is available from the input.

Some theorists have argued that because the information in the retinal image is ambiguous or fragmentary, this bottom-up, data-driven processing would be insufficient to permit the perception of objects, scenes, etc. According to this second view, *stored knowledge* exerts an influence at an early stage in the processing of input, providing additional information which helps to resolve ambiguities or inadequacies in the input, thus permitting suitable interpretations to be made. This type of processing sequence is described as *top-down* and, because it is influenced by stored knowledge, *conceptually-driven*.

This difference between bottom-up, data-driven processing and top-down, conceptually-driven processing is a rather rudimentary way of distinguishing theories about operating principles. Many of the theories to be discussed in the present part imply that processing is not exclusively bottom-up or top-down, but a complex interaction of the two. Other theories show that though 'bottom-up processing' is not influenced by *specific* knowledge about objects or scenes, it is guided by *general* principles about how the physical world is organized. This kind of bottom-up processing can produce complex and informative representations of input with relatively little influence from top-down, conceptually-driven processes.

An assumption common to all these types of theory is that new mental representations constitute the intermediate and final output of perception. The input is assumed to be processed through a number of *stages*, each of which is a new, albeit temporary, representation of the input. The final output of this image processing is a perception which itself represents a real-world object or scene. If this perceptual representation contains novel information, it may be added to that which is already stored. For instance, if you identify a novel type of chair which has folding legs, you may include this information about chairs in your mental representation of the category. There is obviously a close interaction between new mental representations and those which are already stored in memory.

Summary of Section 2.2

- According to the image processing framework, both processes and stored representations play a role in identifying objects from the information in the retinal image.
- Theories can be roughly divided into those which assume bottom-up, data-driven processing, and those which assume top-down, conceptually-driven processing.
- Both types of theory see perception as a sequence of stages in which an input in the form of an image is processed to yield an output in the form of a perception. Each stage including the final output is itself a new representation of the input.

3 The role of features in perceptual processing

What types of information must be extracted from the retinal image of objects if they are to be seen and recognized? Part I discussed the idea that conceptual categories such as 'chair' or 'bird' are mentally represented in terms of the *features* which characterize these categories. It is hardly surprising to find the related idea that recognition of objects results from identification of their component features. But just as Rosch challenged the traditional theory that features represent categories in a clear-cut unambiguous way, so many psychologists now reject the theory that perceptual feature analysis provides adequate unambiguous information for recognizing objects. In evaluating the role of features in perceiving and recognizing objects, we will find many parallels for the difficulties of feature models detailed in Part I.

What do we mean by features? Intuitively, in referring to the features of, say, a chair, we mean components such as arms, legs, back rest. As you will recall from Part I, psychologists such as Rosch have used features in this sense. But as we saw, one problem with adopting these intuitively obvious features as the basic units of mental representation is that they may be broken down or *decomposed* into smaller components which may themselves play an important role in specifying objects. For instance, 'wings' is a feature apparently shared by both birds and bats. But if we list the components (feathers, skin, etc.) of which bird wings or bat wings are made up, we come up with two different feature lists which might provide a basis for discriminating between these two classes of animals. Before concluding that features cannot provide clear-cut unambiguous specifications of objects, one should really seek evidence for *primitive features*, i.e. features of objects which are so basic that they cannot be further decomposed. In a sense this is what physiological studies of feature analysis have attempted to do.

3.1   Are feature detectors part of the hardware?

In a now classic series of studies conducted in the 1950s and 1960s, neurophysiologists such as Hubel and Wiesel (e.g. 1959) studied the responses of single cells in mammalian visual systems to simple light stimuli. In this way they were able to study what types of simple stimuli would be most effective in activating different types of cell. Details of the technique are given in Techniques Box I, which summarizes findings from a number of different studies.

TECHNIQUES BOX I

Studies of Single Cell Responses in the Mammalian Visual System

Rationale
To investigate what types of stimulus are effective in influencing the activity of different types of cell in the visual system.

Method
The activity of single cells in the visual system of an animal such as a cat were electronically monitored. At the same time, a simple light stimulus (e.g. a round spot of light) was projected and moved about on a screen in front of the animal's eyes. Changes from the resting (i.e. unstimulated) activity level of a single cell were recorded as the position of the stimulus on the screen was plotted. This yields a map known as a *receptive field* which defines the shape and size of the area in which this particular cell is influenced by the light stimulus. This procedure is repeated using different shapes of stimulus and recording from cells at different levels in the visual pathways which carry information from the retina to the brain.

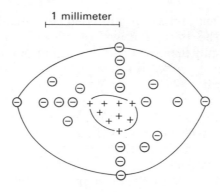

1 millimeter

Figure 2.4   The receptive field for a single ganglion cell. Cells with this type of receptive field are termed on-centre off-surround cells. (Haber and Hershenson, 1973)

Results
Figure 2.4 shows a characteristic receptive field, first described by Kuffler (1953), for a layer of retinal cells known as *ganglion cells*. It contains a central region in which the introduction of a spot of light causes an increase in the rate of firing (i.e. activity) of the cell, after which the level of activity returns to normal. Surrounding this is a larger zone in which the introduction of the light stimulus produces a depression in the rate of firing with a brief burst of activity when the light is turned off. A cell having this type of field is known as an *on-centre off-surround cell*. Some ganglion cells have the opposite off-centre-on-surround kind of receptive field.

Recordings from different parts of the visual system revealed cells whose activity was most readily influenced by different types of stimuli, e.g. light/dark edges instead of spots of light. Each of these types of cell had a characteristic type of receptive field.

SAQ 13
Supposing that one projects a spot of light large enough to cover the entire receptive field shown in Figure 2.4. Do you think such a stimulus would influence the activity of a cell possessing this type of receptive field?

One type of information certainly useful to humans and other mammals is where the boundaries and contours of objects lie. In order to move round a piece of furniture without bumping into it, I need to know where it ends. In order to jump onto the table, a cat needs to know exactly where its edge is. It seemed, therefore, to be no coincidence that one level in the visual pathways beyond the retina was found to contain cells responsive to light/dark *edges*. Yet further up the visual pathways, in part of the brain known as the *visual cortex*, Hubel and Wiesel found cells that were most readily influenced by light/dark edges at particular orientations. For instance, Figure 2.5 shows the nature of the receptive field for a cell known as a *cortical simple cell*, for which a vertically oriented boundary between a dark and a light area is the most effective stimulus.

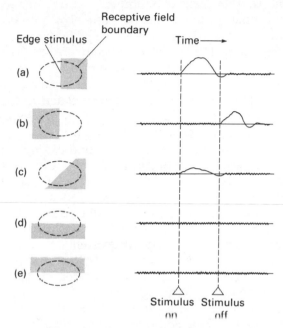

Figure 2.5   Effect on cell activity of an edge stimulus placed at different orientations within the receptive field. With the dark side of the stimulus to the right of the receptive field, there is a burst of activity when the stimulus is introduced (a). But with the dark side to the left, there is a burst of activity when the stimulus is turned off (b). Thus the receptive field consists of one area which is 'on' for light and 'off' for dark, and another which is 'off' for light and 'on' for dark. An edge at 45 degrees to the preferred orientation produces very little change in activity (c), whereas edges at 90 degrees to preferred orientation produce none at all (d) and (e). (Adapted from Oatley, 1972)

At each level in the visual pathways which Hubel and Wiesel investigated, the receptive field properties seemed to elaborate on those at lower levels. For example, some cells resembled cortical simple cells in responding to a line at a particular orientation, but differed in that this line could be placed at *any* point within a large receptive field. Effectively, such cells are relatively insensitive to the retinal position of the image made by the stimulus. This ability to treat as *equivalent* images from different retinal positions is essential if we are to recognize objects from retinal inputs: for example, we can see a square, even though on different viewings it casts an image on very different areas of the retina.

The traditional interpretation of these findings consists of two related proposals. The first is that single cells in the visual system act as *feature detectors*. That is, they extract from the retinal image accurate, unambiguous information about specific features of objects or patterns in the environment. According to this analysis, features such as edges and corners which are detected by these cells are the basic units of analysis from which the visual system synthesizes perceptions of objects. The second proposal is that the visual system is so designed that the output of feature detectors at each level acts as the input for the next level, such that a *hierarchy of feature detectors* analyses increasingly more complex properties of the input.

This classic *feature detection model* is a good example of bottom-up, data-driven processing (see Section 2.2). It could not be directly tested for the human visual system, since single cell recordings require surgical implantation. However, the assumption was that the visual system of humans and other mammals would be sufficiently similar for the same general principles to apply. In addition some indirect methods have been used to investigate the existence of feature detecting cells in humans. If you wish to read more about these you should consult the article by Blakemore in Gregory and Gombrich (1973) listed under Further Reading.

There are some problems with this classic model. First, the notion of a hierarchy of increasingly complex feature detectors implies that there should be a straightforward sequence of anatomical connections between the types of cells investigated, but the actual findings are not entirely consistent with this prediction. However, since these connections are extremely complex, it could be argued that an anatomical basis for the hierarchical model will eventually be discovered.

There is a rather more crucial objection to the notion that single cells act as feature detectors, i.e. provide clear-cut unambiguous information about objects or patterns. For instance, for a cell to be an 'edge-detector' it must respond only to straight light/dark boundaries, and not to any other patterns. But in practice, such cells respond to a large number of other stimuli. Figure 2.6 shows that a cell for which the preferred stimulus is a vertically oriented edge or bar will also respond to stimuli with different properties.

Since the input to the visual system does not usually consist of simple stimuli such as light/dark edges at particular orientations, one cannot predict with any certainty what type of pattern in the real world has activated a particular cell in the visual system. This means that one cannot really think of the cells investigated by Hubel and Wiesel as

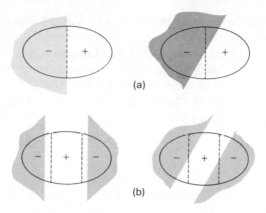

(a)

(b)

Figure 2.6   Ambiguity in the responses of a cortical simple cell. In (a) a low contrast edge at a vertical orientation and a high contrast edge at an oblique orientation evoke the same response. In (b) a vertically oriented slit which is wider than the excitatory region of the cell's receptive field evokes the same response as an oblique slit the same width as the excitatory region. (Adapted from Bruce and Green, 1985)

'feature detectors'. However, the cells in question clearly provide some information which is used by the visual system. David Marr has suggested that the role of these cells can be plausibly reinterpreted in the light of a general theory which specifies what computations the visual system needs to carry out. His account of the role of 'edge detectors' is given in Section 2 of Part III of this volume.

3.2   Is feature analysis a perceptual operating principle?

Leaving aside the 'hardware' involved, is feature analysis one of the processes by which we perceive objects such as chairs or oranges? There is a disappointing lack of direct evidence on this point, since most of the studies which have been carried out have looked at the recognition of printed characters such as letters or numbers. Though this work has had important applications in the design of automatic character recognition devices, it can only provide hints about the processes by which more complex entities such as three-dimensional objects are recognized.

In order to investigate the role of feature analysis in recognizing printed letters, E. Gibson (1969) attempted to specify these characters in terms of simple features such as vertical and horizontal straight lines, curved lines, open and closed loops. She assumed that each character of the alphabet might be uniquely specified by a different combination of these features, but that certain letters would share more features in common than others. For instance, the feature lists for letter pairs such as X and Y should be only slightly different, whereas the feature lists for X and P should be very different. Gibson argued that if subjects (Ss) use features as a basis for recognizing letters, letters sharing similar feature lists would be more likely to be confused with one another in tasks where Ss are given insufficient time to process all the available features. A test of this prediction is described in Techniques Box J.

TECHNIQUES BOX J

The use of features in recognizing letters (Gibson, 1969)

Rationale
To study the errors made by Ss in recognizing printed letters. If Ss use features such as vertical and horizontal lines to recognize letters, letters sharing many common features should be more often confused with one another when Ss are given insufficient time to process all the available information.

Method
Ss were shown individual printed letters for a fraction of a second in a tachistoscope and asked to identify the letters with maximum speed and accuracy. *Confusion errors* were recorded, i.e. the number of times each letter is confused with each other letter in the alphabet.

Results
Confusion errors were summarized in a *confusion matrix*, which shows whether particular letters are regularly confused with one another. The most often confused letters were found to be the ones which share many of the features defined by Gibson, e.g. 'b' and 'p' were regularly confused with one another, whereas 'b' and 'x' were not.

Further studies revealed a somewhat more complex pattern of results, since it was found that sound as well as appearance determines which letters are confused. However, similar effects of visual confusion have been obtained in *visual search* tasks where Ss are asked to search through an array of letters for a particular letter (e.g. Neisser, 1963). Ss perform this task more quickly and more accurately when the letter is embedded in an array of letters sharing few 'features' with it.

SAQ 14
(a) What letters would you expect to be most often confused with the letter C?
(b) What array of letters would make searching for a letter N easy?

The classic interpretation of these results runs directly parallel to the classic interpretation of Hubel and Wiesel's results discussed in the previous section. Letter features such as horizontal lines or loops are assumed to provide clear-cut unambiguous information from which letters may be recognized provided there is sufficient time to process all the available information. The 'feature analysers' which extract these lines and loops are assumed to provide the first stage in a hierarchy of analysers which extract successively more complex features until eventually a letter can be recognized. Details of models based on these proposals will be found in many textbooks—see for instance Bruce and Green (1985).

Limitations of this feature model are apparent even in the case of printed character recognition. For instance, we can construct examples in which the identity of a printed character is ambiguous—it cannot be resolved by feature analysis alone. In Figure 2.7 the middle letters of both words are identical, and should therefore activate the same set of feature detectors. Yet we see one letter as an H and the other as an A.

Figure 2.7   T H E   C H T

In this example the surrounding *context* of the letters evokes *expectations* which influence how the letters are seen.

This is a clear example in which bottom-up, data-driven processing (detecting the features of the letters) must be supplemented by top-down, conceptually-driven processing (using the context to interpret the letter).

Another problem for feature analysis as an explanation of printed character recognition is that subjects in tachistoscopic recognition tasks confuse letters not only on the basis of their component features, but also on the basis of overall shape (Lupker, 1979). This suggests that when people read printed characters they process the overall shape of letters as well as, or even instead, of their individual features.

A further difficulty for the feature theory is that some letters (e.g. b and d) actually share the same features. According to feature theory, such letters should be indistinguishable. The fact that such letters are readily distinguished in everyday life implies that the relationship between the features (the way the features are put together) is important in identifying letters as well as the features themselves.

If feature analysis is insufficient to account for all of the phenomena of printed character recognition, the limitations must be even greater for more complex perceptual tasks—such as how we read handwriting, recognize people's faces, articles of furniture, etc. For instance, whereas Figure 2.7 was specially constructed to illustrate the problems of ambiguity and fragmentary data, these are natural properties of handwriting. You may be aware of using the same stroke of the pen for two different letters. The identity of the pen stroke will be clear to a reader from the surrounding context of letters. In many people's handwriting, certain letters appear as little more than a squiggle — yet their identity is inferred when reading whole words or sentences.

For these complex perceptual tasks, the underlying problem of recognition by feature analysis is that it is impossible to *define* complex entities in terms of their component features. This was discussed in detail in Part I.

Each of the problems raised by the feature hypothesis points to an alternative theory which is introduced somewhere in the present volume. The rationale for these alternative theories is given in Table 2.1, together with the places where they are discussed. You may find it useful to refer to this table when reading these other sections.

Table 2.1

Problem with feature hypothesis	Alternative approach	See	
Features may be ambiguous or insufficient for recognizing patterns or objects.	(1) More complex information is extracted bottom-up from the retinal image.	Perceptual grouping	Sections 4.1, 4.2
		Marr's approach	Part III
	(2) Processing the retinal image is guided by the top-down influence of stored knowledge.	Uncon-scious inferences	Sections 5.1, 5.2
Recognition may be based on overall shape rather than specific features.	Global or wholistic properties of patterns are extracted from the retinal image.	Processing of wholistic properties	Sections 4.3, 4.4
Patterns or objects having the same features put together in different ways can be recognized and discriminated.	Not just features but relationships among features are important in specifying patterns and objects.	Structural descriptions model	Section 6.1
Patterns or objects can be recognized even if they cannot be clearly defined in terms of component features.	Patterns and objects are represented by prototypes or typical feature lists.	Rosch's approach	Part I

Summary of Section 3

- Neurophysiological studies have provided evidence for cells whose activity can be influenced by different types of light stimulus. The classic interpretation of these findings is that the visual system contains feature detectors hierarchically arranged to extract increasingly complex features of input.
- The classic model is questioned by the absence of appropriate cell connections, and by the fact that several different shapes of stimulus can influence the activity of a given cell.
- The inadequacy of the feature hypothesis even for tasks such as printed character recognition makes it necessary to consider alternative more complex operating principles.

4   *Perceptual organization*

We seem to perceive objects as structured coherent wholes rather more readily than we perceive their component parts. In this section I shall consider the processes by which discrete components of objects, such as the features discussed in the last section, are perceptually grouped together. An important aspect of this discussion concerns whether the *global* or *wholistic* properties of inputs take precedence in perception over local details, as our introspections suggest. First, however, we shall consider the basic phenomena of perceptual grouping.

4.1   *Perceptual grouping: the Gestalt approach*

The most comprehensive account of *perceptual grouping* is still that provided by the *Gestalt* psychologists in the 1920s. They are best known for their claim that 'the whole is greater than the sum of the parts'. This refers to the fact that figures are seen as organized structures which have properties not found in the component parts—so-called *emergent properties*. A main theme of their research was a set of *laws* describing what types of perceptual structures are systematically evoked by particular types of pattern. Figure 2.8 illustrates a combination of some of these laws.

First, the dots are seen as lines rather than unconnected points because they are close to one another and similar to one another,

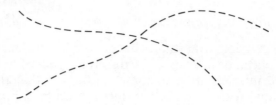

Figure 2.8   Illustration of the Gestalt laws of proximity, similarity and good continuity

illustrating the laws of *proximity* and *similarity*. Secondly, these lines are seen as two smooth curves crossing in the middle, rather than as two 'Vs' meeting at a point. This is because it is the former structure which preserves smooth continuity rather than yielding an abrupt change, illustrating the law of *good continuity*. Individual laws such as these were held by the Gestalt psychologists to be manifestations of a more basic *Law of Pragnanz*, which Koffka (1935) described as follows: 'Of several geometrically possible organizations, that one will actually occur which possesses the best, simplest and most stable shape'.

SAQ 15
The pattern shown in Figure 2.9 might be structured in each of the following ways:

(a) A square
(b) A cross
(c) A triangle plus dot
Which of these structures do you think conforms to the Law of Pragnanz? Was this how you actually saw the figure?

Figure 2.9

As you probably realize, this begs the question of what is meant by the 'best structure', but more recent research has attempted to provide an objective basis for the Gestalt laws. For a fuller account of the laws themselves, see Bruce and Green (1985).

The Gestalt laws are still accepted as descriptions of grouping phenomena. However, they have limited explanatory value. For one thing the Gestalt psychologists did not test their laws experimentally. Their claim that a particular figure was perceptually structured in a particular way was based on the *phenomenological method*—what has been termed the 'look at the figure and see for yourself' method. This method tells us that Figure 2.8 looks like two continuous curves intersecting one another, but it does not tell us what perceptual processes are involved, nor how similar or how near the dots have to be to be seen in this way. A second problem with the laws is that they are difficult to apply to the perception of solid objects. We have no difficulty in perceiving that the parts of an object such as a chair 'go together', but which of the Gestalt laws accounts for this type of perceptual grouping? Finally, there has proved to be no basis for the Gestaltist's claim that perceptual organization is produced by brain forces structurally similar to what is perceived. According to this theory we see Figure 2.10a as an ellipse because an elliptical-shaped pattern of excitation is set up in the brain.

(a)   (b)

Figure 2.10   The shape in (a) is seen as an ellipse. In (b) the context is such that the object held by the boy is seen as circular. (Adapted from Gregory, 1973)

Even if this theory was physiologically sound, it does not explain why the identical shape in Figure 2.10b is seen as circular. The Gestalt theory made no allowance for the way in which interpretations of sensory data are influenced by learned knowledge about what patterns are most probable in particular contexts.

To conclude, the legacy of the Gestalt movement is detailed *descriptions* rather than *explanations* of organizational phenomena observed with 2-dimensional figures. It is only in more recent work that explanations for these phenomena have been sought within the framework of cognitive psychology and Artificial Intelligence.

4.2   Recent approachs to perceptual grouping

Pomerantz (1981) has reviewed a number of experiments which provide objective measures of perceptual grouping. He argues that if a set of elements lend themselves to perceptual grouping then Ss should have difficulty in responding to one element of the set while ignoring others. Conversely, if a set of elements do not lend themselves to grouping, it should be easy to respond to one member of the set while ignoring others. One objective measure of grouping is thus how quickly Ss can sort or *classify* one element presented with others which the S must try to ignore (see Techniques Box K).

TECHNIQUES BOX K

An Experimental Measure of Perceptual Grouping (Pomerantz and Garner, 1973)

Rationale
To demonstrate that if a set of elements form a perceptual group, it is difficult to classify one element while ignoring the others.

Method
Ss were given a pile of cards each with a pair of brackets printed on it — see Figure 2.11 for examples. Ss were asked to sort the cards into two piles (A and B) according to whether the left-hand bracket on each card looks like this '(' or like this ')'. Ss were told to ignore the right-hand bracket completely in carrying out the task. In one condition the pairs of elements were predicted to be *groupable* whereas in the other they were predicted to be *non-groupable*. In each condition there was an experimental and a control pack. Figure 2.11 shows examples of groupable and non-groupable elements from both experimental and control packs. The right-hand column summarizes the predictions for each condition.

Results
As predicted, when cards had 'groupable' elements on them Ss were slow in sorting the experimental pack, implying that they were unable

---

to ignore the variations in the irrelevant right-hand bracket. When cards had non-groupable elements there was no difference in the times taken to sort experimental and control packs, implying that Ss were able to ignore variations in the irrelevant right-hand bracket.

		Sort into pile A B B A	Predictions
Groupable stimuli	Control	(( ) ( ) (((	Ss will group these stimuli ∴ they will have difficulty ignoring right-hand bracket. Sorting speed for control pack will be relatively unaffected since right-hand bracket always the same, but sorting speed for experimental pack will be slow since right-hand bracket varies.
	Experimental	(( ) ( )) ( )	
Non-groupable stimuli	Control	(⌐)⌐)⌐ (⌐	Ss will not group these elements ∴ they will ignore right-hand bracket in sorting cards. Thus, no difference in sorting speed between control condition (right-hand bracket constant) and experimental condition (right-hand bracket varies)
	Experimental	(⌐)⌐)⌐ (⌐	

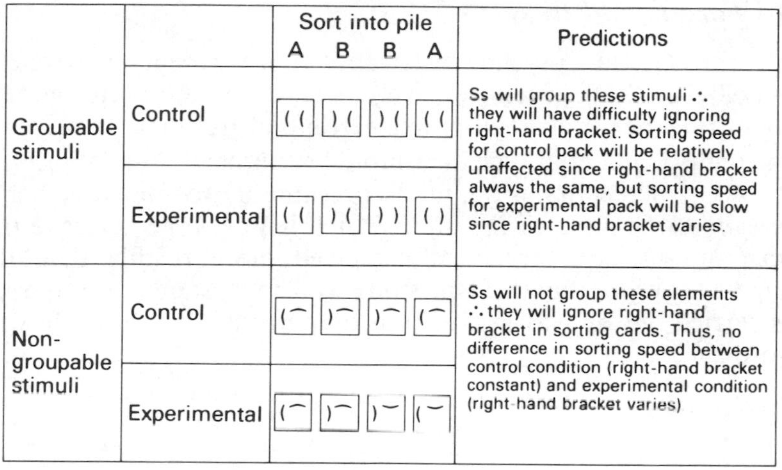

Figure 2.11

The value of this study is to show that there are objective correlates for the perceptual phenomenon of grouping. Elements which are seen as grouped are also processed differently from elements which are not seen as grouped. In Pomerantz and Garner's study the grouped elements were processed less efficiently (i.e. more slowly) because Ss were trying to select out one element from a group. Under conditions where Ss are required to attend to all elements of a group, groupable elements are processed more efficiently—see Pomerantz (1981) for further discussion.

Having established objective correlates of perceptual grouping one can begin to investigate the basis of the Gestalt laws. For instance, what is it about the groupable elements in Figure 2.11 which makes them groupable? The Gestalt laws imply that *proximity* and *similarity* should be involved. In a study by Pomerantz and Schwaitzberg (1975) proximity was systematically manipulated by using cards with the brackets drawn further and further apart. Given a suitable separation between the paired elements, the grouping effects were found to disappear, i.e. there was no longer a difference between the times taken to classify experimental and control pairs of 'groupable' stimuli. While this experiment shows that proximity is partly responsible for the grouping effect, a study by Olson and Attneave (1970) implies that similarity in the orientation of the 'groupable' elements is also important.

4.3   Forests and trees

Both the Gestalt psychologists and more recent experimental psychologists have used relatively simple patterns in order to demonstrate the variables governing perceptual grouping. In perceiving more realistic material such as complex patterns or solid objects, the purpose of perceptual grouping is presumably to 'put together' or *segregate* those parts of the input which belong together. Are these *global* or *wholistic* structures perceived more readily than their components or *local parts*? One study which investigates this question was carried out by Navon (1977) using patterns like those shown in Figure 2.12.

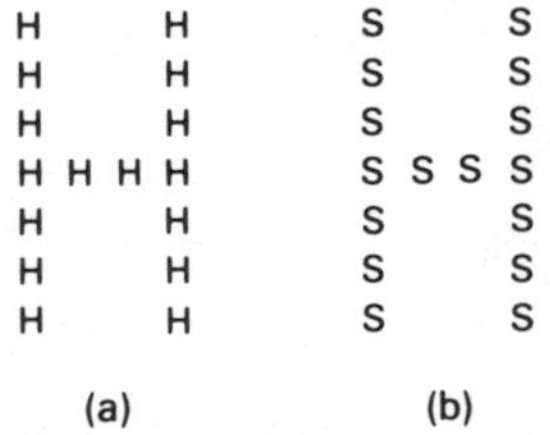

```
H       H        S       S
H       H        S       S
H       H        S       S
H H H H          S S S S
H       H        S       S
H       H        S       S
H       H        S       S

   (a)                (b)
```

Figure 2.12   In (a) local and global elements match. In (b) they mismatch

Each large letter in Figure 2.12 is a *global configuration* made up of *local elements*. The global configuration and the local elements either match or mismatch one another. Navon argued that if the global configuration (the large letter) is processed more readily than its component parts (the smaller letters) then the mismatch between the configuration and the elements will not affect processing of the global configuration, but will affect processing of the local elements. A test of this hypothesis is described in Techniques Box L.

Navon concluded from these results that global configurations are processed more readily than their component parts. However, Pomerantz (1981) argues that this conclusion is too inflexible since the relative precedence of global v. local processing may depend on the viewing conditions and the nature of the task. It seems obvious that in everyday life it is sometimes easier to process 'forests' and sometimes it is easier to process 'trees'.

TECHNIQUES BOX L

Global Superiority in Processing Letters (Navon, 1977)

Rationale
To investigate whether a global configuration is processed more readily than its component parts. If so, a conflict between the global configuration and its local elements should only affect processing of the local elements.

Method
Ss were presented with stimuli like those in Figure 2.12. For half the stimuli there was a match between large and small elements (as in Figure 2.12a) and for half there was a mismatch (as in Figure 2.12b). Ss were asked to identify which letter they had seen by pressing one key for H and another key for S. In the *global* condition Ss were instructed to identify the large letter and ignore its component letters. In the *local* condition Ss were instructed to identify the small letters and ignore the global letter.

Results
Table 2.2 shows that Ss responded significantly faster in the 'global' condition than in the 'local' condition. In the global conditions Ss' reaction times were the same whether the large and small letters matched or not. In the local condition Ss responded much more slowly when the letters mismatched than when they matched. This suggests that in the global condition Ss were able to ignore the local elements, whereas in the local condition they were unable to ignore the global pattern.

Table 2.2   Times (in milliseconds) to respond to 'global' letters or 'local' letters

| Condition | Type of stimulus | |
	Large and small letters match	Large and small letters mismatch
Global	471	477
Local	581	664

4.4   Processing wholes and parts

It is clearly useful to distinguish between processing which commences with local details and builds up to global configurations (*local-to-global processing*) and processing which commences with the global configuration and proceeds to an analysis of local detail (*global-to-local processing*). How does this distinction relate to the one drawn earlier between bottom-up, data-driven and top-down conceptually driven processing?

One model which is easy to classify on both dimensions is the classic hierarchical feature analysis model, a clear example of bottom-up, data-driven processing.

SAQ 16
Would you characterize feature analysis as local-to-global or global-to-local?

In this example, bottom-up, data-driven processing clearly implies starting with local details (the features) and building up to a complex configuration (a representation of a figure or object). But our discussion of wholistic phenomena suggests that the two distinctions do not always align in this way.

The phenomena of perceptual organization are often assumed to reflect bottom-up, data-driven processing. That is, the processing is guided by properties of the sensory input, such as proximity and similarity of elements. However, this bottom-up processing sequence does not necessarily commence with local details. As we have seen, processing may be local-to-global or global-to-local depending on the viewing conditions and the task.

Perceptual organization is not invariably the result of bottom-up processing. In fact, both bottom-up and top-down processing can produce surprisingly similar 'elaborations' of the data in the retinal image. For instance, Figure 2.13a shows an arrangement of four lines which is seen as a square, even though the lines do not meet one another. In Figure 2.13b, the central arrangement of lines is seen as a B, though again the lines do not meet and could equally represent the number 13.

(a)   (b)

Figure 2.13

Both figures are, in a sense, illustrations of the Gestalt *law of closure*, according to which gaps in figures are closed to yield 'good' perceptions. Yet the underlying processes may be different. In Figure 2.13a, the data may be processed bottom-up simply by applying the rule that lines juxtaposed in this way are likely to belong together and should therefore be joined up. This processing is bottom-up because knowledge of what the figure is likely to be is not needed to yield the perception of a square. In contrast, for Figure 2.13b, stored knowledge that the central character is more likely to be a B than a 13, given the context, exerts a top-down influence on how the data is interpreted. This example makes the important point that one cannot always distinguish bottom-up and top-down processing by the complexity of what they can achieve.

One wholistic phenomenon which clearly reflects the influence of stored knowledge is the *word superiority effect*. Single letters such as D are more accurately identified if they have previously been presented within a word such as LOAD, rather than a non-word anagram (DLAO), or on their own. This appears to show that people can process whole words more efficiently than any of their component letters. Similar effects have been reported for pictures of objects.

The force of these observations is that the processing of organized wholistic properties reflects a complex combination of processing modes. Processing may be local-to-global or global-to-local. Processing may be bottom-up and use grouping according to set rules to 'elaborate' the data in the retinal image. Alternatively, this elaboration may be influenced top-down by stored knowledge of the properties of configurations. Figure 2.14 illustrates a complex interaction of all of these processing modes.

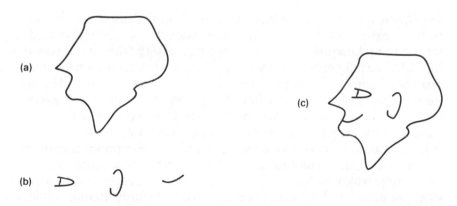

Figure 2.14   The perceptual data in (a) and in (b) only make sense when seen in relation to each other, as in (c). Thus the global outline in (a) acts as a context which provides top-down guidance for the interpretation of the ambiguous data in (b). But the local elements in (b) serve precisely the same function in interpreting the ambiguous data in (a). This suggests a cyclical combination of top-down and bottom-up, local-to-global and global-to-local processing. (Adapted from Palmer, 1975)

Summary of Section 4

- The Gestalt laws describe some of the ways in which elements of patterns are grouped into wholes having emergent properties not found in the original elements.
- Recent work on perceptual organization has suggested objective measures for grouping, such as the time taken to process grouped *v.* ungrouped elements.
- Global properties sometimes, but not always, take precedence over local details in processing.
- The processing of patterns as wholes implies a complex interaction of bottom-up and top-down, local-to-global and global-to-local operating principles.

5   Unconscious inference and direct perception

One question which has remained implicit in the discussion so far is to what extent the input to the visual system must be elaborated if we are to make sense of it. The image processing framework sees the input for visual perception as a two-dimensional retinal image which provides fragmentary, often inadequate *cues* for perception. This has led some psychologists to conclude that perception is an *indirect process* in which these sensory cues are used to draw *inferences* about the world. Rather in the way that a detective constructs an account of a crime from the limited cues available to him, so perception consists in constructing 'interpretations' from whatever sensory cues are available. To explain why we are largely unaware that inferences are occurring when we perceive things, they are assumed to be *unconscious*, an idea originally proposed in the nineteenth century by Helmholtz.

Inferential processing is usually thought to rely heavily on the top-down influence of stored knowledge acquired through learning. In practice, however, there are several kinds of inference, not all of which work in the same way. We shall consider two sources of evidence for inferences before turning to a theory which contrasts strongly with the inferential view.

5.1   Contextual effects

There is considerable evidence that *contextual* information plays a part in recognizing patterns such as letters or words from deficient or ambiguous sensory data (see Figure 2.13b for example). Techniques Box M describes a more unusual study by Palmer (1975) of how context, in the form of a pictorial scene, affects recognition of familiar objects presented very briefly on a screen.

TECHNIQUES BOX M

The Effect of Contextual Scenes on the Recognition of Objects (Palmer, 1975)

Rationale
To investigate whether the recognition of familiar objects, presented as pictures, is affected by prior presentation of a contextual scene. If so, Ss should identify objects more accurately after seeing an appropriate contextual scene, than after seeing an inappropriate contextual scene, or no scene at all.

Method
Ss were shown slides giving contextual information, each followed by a picture of an object which they had to identify—see Figure 2.15 overleaf for examples.

Table 2.3 summarizes the four contextual conditions.

Table 2.3

Condition	Scene	Object
Appropriate context	Kitchen	Loaf
No context	Blank	Loaf
Inappropriate context/ Similar object	Kitchen	Mailbox (looks like loaf)
Inappropriate context/ Different object	Kitchen	Drum (does not look like loaf)

The prediction was that the 'appropriate context' condition would enhance identification of the objects compared to the 'no context' condition, whereas the 'inappropriate context' conditions would impair identification relative to the 'no context' condition. The 'inappropriate context/similar object' condition should be particularly confusing. The context, in conjunction with the ambiguous sensory data from the object, should point to 'loaf' rather than 'mailbox'.

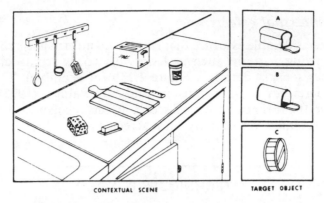

CONTEXTUAL SCENE   TARGET OBJECT

Figure 2.15   An example of a slide showing a contextual scene, with examples of objects to be identified

Results
The probability of correctly identifying an object was highest when it was preceded by an appropriate scene, lower when preceded by no context, and lower still when preceded by an inappropriate context. As predicted the 'inappropriate context/similar object' condition was inferior to the 'inappropriate context/different object' condition. In addition, Ss frequently confused objects in the visually similar pairs, e.g. giving 'loaf' instead of 'mailbox' after seeing the kitchen scene.

These results imply that the contextual information influenced Ss expectations as to what object they would see, and thus affected the inferences they drew from sensory data. Our stored knowledge of what to find in a kitchen leads us to expect a loaf rather than a mailbox and thus to interpret the sensory data in this way. Obviously, if the data conflict completely with the expectation (a drum does not look at all like a loaf) it will not be so readily misidentified.

There are several different ways in which context may influence sensory analysis. For instance, in processing the word 'mat' within a sentence such as 'the cat sat on the mat', the expectations aroused by the first five words may permit Ss to analyse fewer features of the word 'mat' then if it was presented without a context (Rumelhart, 1977). In this case, the context permits perceptual processing to be more selective. Some studies suggest that while Ss process all the available stimulus information, rather than selecting from it, contextual information enhances this processing, making it faster and/or more accurate. For instance, in processing the sentence 'the cat sat on the mat', the first five words may prime the memory representation for 'mat', such that the word is more rapidly identified (Meyer *et al.*, 1975).

Palmer favoured a version of this explanation for the results described in Techniques Box M. He suggested that the enhancing effect of the appropriate context was to make the correct name for the object more readily available from memory.

Contextual effects do not invariably reflect the top-down influence of stored knowledge. In the study of grouping described in Techniques Box K, the irrelevant brackets can be thought of as a context which influences Ss' ability to process the relevant bracket. In Figure 2.14 the overall shape provides a context in which individual lines can be made sense of. Such grouping processes are assumed to operate bottom-up and are not usually thought of as 'inferential'. Yet there is a broad sense in which the visual system 'infers' organized patterns from the inputs which it receives.

5.2   *Visual illusions*

If perception is inferential rather than direct, it should sometimes generate mistakes or paradoxes, which is precisely what *visual illusions* are. Richard Gregory (1973) has made extensive use of visual illusions to support his view that perceptions are *hypotheses* which are tested against sensory data, much in the way that *scientific hypotheses* are tested against experimental data. Visual illusions reflect the erroneous or misplaced hypotheses which inevitably occur among the usually appropriate hypotheses of perception. A good example is provided by the *Ponzo perspective illusion* illustrated in Figure 2.16. The upper of the two horizontal lines is seen as longer than the lower, though the two are in fact the same length.

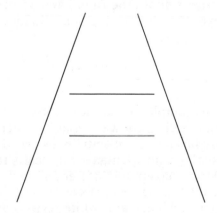

Figure 2.16   The Ponzo perspective illusion

A convincing explanation of this illusion is in terms of *inappropriate constancy scaling*. Constancy scaling is the process by which the same object viewed at different distances is seen to preserve the same size even though it produces retinal images of quite different sizes (see Figure 2.17).

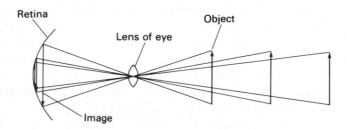

Figure 2.17 The retinal image cast by a single object becomes smaller as the distance between object and eye increases

According to Gregory, this constancy scaling is triggered by *cues* indicating depth. These cues are used by the visual system to infer that the relatively small retinal image signifies an object of the same size as the larger retinal image of a similar object seen close to. Thus the perception of object size remains more or less constant for different viewing distances.

The presence of *depth cues* in a scene which has no actual depth may trigger inappropriate constancy scaling, and this is what seems to happen in the Ponzo illustration. The two tapering lines appear to act as cues for distance, rather as if they represented railway lines receding into the distance. The visual system adopts this three-dimensional hypothesis about the figure and accordingly 'scales up' the length of the upper line as if it were more distant than the lower line.

SAQ 17
Why do you think that people, cars etc. look tiny when seen from the window of a plane?

Notice that in these examples we cannot choose to perceive the input to the visual system in a different way — our interpretation is not under conscious control. Thus we do not actually see any depth in the Ponzo figure, but the visual system spontaneously scales the lines as if they were in depth. Most perceptual inferences seem to work in this unconscious way, although there are exceptions. For instance, Figure 2.2 showed a pattern of black and white regions which can be seen as a dog, but at first only with a conscious effort. Gregory argues that both types of inference reflect hypotheses based on stored assumptions about the significance of particular cues. The point is that most perceptual hypotheses occur spontaneously at a stage in visual processing over which we have no conscious control, whereas some can be consciously influenced. Paradoxically, then, Gregory sees inference and hypothesis as fundamental operating principles which frequently work 'directly' on sensory input. How far does this idea really differ from the theory of *direct perception* proposed by J. J. Gibson?

5.3   Direct perception?

The theory of direct perception (J. J. Gibson, 1979) contrasts (at least philosophically) with almost all the assumptions of the image processing framework which have underpinned our discussion so far.

To recap, the image processing framework sees the basic input for visual perception as a two-dimensional retinal image (or equivalent representation in an artificial vision system). There are of course different views about the information which this image provides, but there is general agreement that the information is partial, ambiguous or in a raw form. According to this view, processes are required to transform this information into a form which can be made sense of. Our discussion has shown that these processes can be of different kinds — bottom-up or top-down, local-to-global or global-to-local, automatic or consciously controlled. Again, there is general agreement that these processes transform the retinal input through a series of intermediate stages or representations. Finally, there is agreement that previously stored knowledge plays a role in making sense of the retinal input, though there are different views as to how and when this influence occurs.

Gibson sees the input for visual perception not as a 2-dimensional retinal image, but as a complex pattern of light which is specifically structured by the surfaces from which it has been reflected. Different types of surface reflect light in different ways. For instance the surface of a leaf reflects less red light and more green light than a poppy which reflects less green light and more red light. A smooth surface such as a mirror reflects light more uniformly than a natural surface such as wood bark, which reflects light unevenly. All this information is 'captured' in the pattern of light which reaches the observer's eye.

This pattern, known as the *optic array*, can be thought of as a number of tiny cone-shaped beams, each coming to a point at the observer's eye, and each containing a different mixture of wavelength, texture and other information. According to Gibson, this optic array provides *invariant* information about the world. That is, it specifies the layout of objects in space in an unambiguous fashion, which can be directly 'picked up' by the perceiver. Imagine that you are looking across the floor to the edge of your room. The texture of the floor covering (wool carpet, cork tiles, stripped wood, etc.) will reflect light in a characteristic way. Moreover there will be systematic changes in this pattern of reflected light along the line of sight from your eye to the wall, yielding what Gibson calls a *texture gradient*. Since all of this patterning is part of the optic array, it will provide unambiguous and direct information about the location of the wall, the position of objects on the floor etc. Figure 2.18 gives some examples of texture gradients, which give the impression of surfaces receding into the distance.

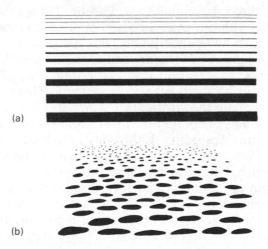

Figure 2.18   Examples of texture gradients. The relative compression and diminution of the lines in (a) and the spots in (b) give the impression of surfaces receding into the distance

SAQ 18
What would be the role of texture gradients such as those in Figure 2.18 in Gregory's theory of constancy scaling?

So far we have considered what information the optic array makes available for a static observer. Gibson points out that a further major source of information is available because the organism and sometimes its surroundings are moving. With movement, the pattern of light reflected from surfaces changes in its relation to the organism. This sets up characteristic dynamic patterns in the optic array, which Gibson describes by the term *optic flow*. To get an idea of what is meant by optic flow, imagine yourself looking out of the back of a moving train. It seems as if the track, countryside etc. are flowing away from you,

Figure 2.19 The optic flow pattern for a person looking out of the back of a train. (Bruce and Green, 1985)

as illustrated in Figure 2.19. As with texture gradients, the claim is that the organism has direct unambiguous information about its movement relative to the environment.

To summarize, according to Gibson the total information in the optic array is so rich and complex it provides a direct basis for a person's interactions with the world. There is no need for processes to transform the input into intermediate representations or to supplement it by drawing on stored knowledge. In essence, our interactions with the environment can proceed without any need for information processing.

In the short space available it is impossible to do full justice to such a complex theory (or its critics!). If you are interested in pursuing it further you should consult Gibson, J. J. (1979) or Bruce and Green (1985). Just a few main 'pros' and 'cons' of the theory will be mentioned here.

Gibson's theory seems particularly suited to explaining perception in skilled tasks such as a pilot landing a plane or a tennis player returning a shot. In these situations the perceiver must have precise information which can be directly translated into immediate action. The theory is similarly suited to explaining some of the perceptual behaviour of animals. For instance, a seagull must be able to swoop down and catch a fish which is seen only momentarily at the surface of the water. Again, precise unambiguous information must be translated into immediate action.

113

However, there are other phenomena which the theory is less suited to explain. For instance, if the optic array contains such accurate information about the layout of the environment it is not clear why illusions should occur. Gibson's answer to this criticism is that most illusions are an unfair test of what the visual system can do with information from the natural environment. However, there are illusions which occur despite the rich information available in natural settings. For instance, if you stare for some time at a waterfall and then transfer your gaze to a stationary object, the object will appear to drift in the opposite direction, while paradoxically seeming to maintain its position relative to the surroundings. Gibson's theory does not explain such naturally occurring illusions. (The waterfall illusion is probably due to selective fatigue of a movement-detecting system.)

Another area in which Gibson's theory seems inadequate is in handling the more high-level categorical aspects of perception. According to Gibson an object such as a chair 'affords' direct information about its function and properties. There is apparently no need to consult stored knowledge about chairs since the necessary information (e.g. that chairs are for sitting on) can be 'picked up' from the object itself. However, it seems extremely implausible that this idea of *affordance* could be elaborated to explain how for instance we recognize a Chippendale chair similar to one that Aunt Mabel had in her front room years ago.

Arguments such as these suggest that Gibson's theory should be viewed as complementary to the other approaches we have discussed rather than as a substitute for them. The most useful insight he has offered is that there is more information in the input to the visual system than has been traditionally assumed. You will find this influence in the work of David Marr, who none the less retains many of the general assumptions of the image processing approach. His own assessment of Gibson is as follows:

> Gibson asked the critically important question. How does one obtain constant perceptions in everyday life on the basis of continually changing sensations? This is exactly the right question, showing that Gibson correctly regarded the problem of perception as that of recovering from sensory information 'valid' properties of the external world . . .
>
> Although one can criticize certain shortcomings in the quality of Gibson's analysis, its major and, in my view, fatal shortcoming lies at a deeper level and results from a failure to realize two things. First, the detection of physical invariants, like image surfaces, is exactly and precisely an information-processing problem, in modern terminology. And second, he vastly underrated the sheer difficulty of such detection.   (Marr, 1982, p. 30)

Finally, the contrast between Gibson and other theorists is accentuated by differences in philosophy and semantic usage. Gibson used the term 'direct perception' to contrast it with the 'inferential' view. Yet as you will recall, Gregory sees many inferences as operating in a direct and spontaneous fashion—a view which shares something in common with Gibson's approach.

Summary of Section 5

- According to the inferential theory of perception, sensory input provides fragmentary or ambiguous cues, which are used to construct inferences or hypotheses about objects or patterns.
- The fact that contextual information enhances the perception of fragmentary or ambiguous data supports the inferential view.
- The fact that sensory data can be misinterpreted, leading to visual illusions, also supports the inferential view.
- Many inferences are spontaneous and outside conscious control. Others are influenced by conscious effort.
- Gibson has argued that perception is direct rather than inferential, and has rejected the main assumptions of the image processing approach.
- Gibson's theory is particularly suited to explaining the perceptual achievements of both humans and other animals in skilled tasks requiring immediate action e.g. playing tennis, catching prey. It has difficulties in explaining why illusions occur and how we attach complex meanings to input.

6 Perceptual representation

Though our discussion has so far centred on the processes of visual perception, it has made clear that these processes interact closely with *representations*—both new representations of input and those already stored in memory. For instance, a process such as feature analysis requires stored representations of features with which the newly extracted features can be compared. If the extracted features provide ambiguous information about the pattern or object, stored representations provide hypotheses about what it might be. The outcomes of feature matches or hypothesis testing are themselves new representations—either intermediate representations, such as the lines and angles extracted from an image, or the final output such as a perception of an object.

What type of representation is adequate for the task of seeing and making sense of two-dimensional patterns or three-dimensional objects? Traditional feature models (see Part I and Section 3 of this Part) are inadequate because they assume that objects or patterns can be unambiguously specified or defined by a list of their component features. In practice, complex patterns such as handwriting, as well as real objects such as chairs, are difficult or impossible to specify in this way. Part I considered the solutions which Rosch proposed to this problem. The prototype model assumed that categories of objects are not represented by features at all, but by single composite entities based on typical category members. Difficulties in defining what these prototypes might be led Rosch to the alternative proposal that object categories are represented by features associated with typical category members. This allows for the fact that not all chairs seem to share precisely the same set of features. However, neither the traditional feature model, nor this revised version places enough emphasis on how features are put together. For instance, the object in Figure 2.20 shares many of the features of typical chairs (four legs, back rest, etc.), yet is seen as an extremely atypical chair or non-chair.

Figure 2.20   'Can-can chair' (Source: Carelman, 1971)

The trouble with this joke 'chair' is that its features or parts have been put together in the wrong way, with the result that it could not readily be used for sitting on! This implies that the structural relationships among parts of a pattern or object may be an important criterion in perceiving or categorizing it correctly. In fact some psychologists believe that these *structural descriptions* provide the kind of unambiguous specification which traditional feature theories have failed to produce, and which Rosch has rejected out of hand.

6.1   Structural descriptions

Formally speaking, a structural description is a set of *propositions** about a pattern from which the actual pattern may be generated. It consists of the parts of the pattern, together with the rules for linking them up, which are necessary to reconstruct the pattern. Exactly the same definition applies to objects, which for these purposes can be thought of as complex three-dimensional patterns.

SAQ 19
Consider the letters 'b', 'd' and 'p'. A simple feature list (straight vertical line and closed loop) is the same for all three letters and could not provide a basis for distinguishing between them.

Imagine that you are describing these letters to a friend who has to identify them from your description or write them on paper. What is the minimum information which your friend needs about each letter?

The answers to SAQ 19 consist of simple structural descriptions. They represent the letters in terms of features, together with rules defining the structural relationships between the features.

A psychological theory based round the idea of structural descriptions assumes that previously encountered patterns or objects are mentally represented as structural descriptions. New patterns or objects are themselves converted into structural descriptions in order to be recognized.

Reed (e.g. 1973, 1974) has suggested a formal system of structural descriptions for geometric figures such as the one shown in Figure 2.21.

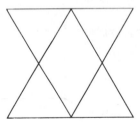

Figure 2.21   Example of geometric figure used in Reed's studies

He has also investigated how people actually store this kind of pattern and how they recognize newly presented patterns, using a task known as the *embedded figures task*. Reed argued that if Ss store the

*Propositional representations are discussed in the articles by Rumelhart and Norman, and Kosslyn in Aitkenhead and Slack (eds) (1985).

patterns as structural descriptions, they will find it easy to identify shapes which are part of these structural descriptions, and difficult to identify shapes which, though part of the pattern, are not part of the structural descriptions.

It is of course possible that Ss do not store the patterns as structural descriptions at all, but as *templates* which can be thought of as mirroring the form of the whole pattern in a one-to-one fashion. In this case though, Ss should not find some pattern parts more difficult to identify than others. A test of these hypotheses is described in Techniques Box N.

TECHNIQUES BOX N

An Embedded Figures Study of How People Represent Geometric Patterns (Reed, 1974)

Rationale
To investigate whether Ss represent geometric patterns as structural descriptions. If so, Ss will find it easy to identify shapes which are part of their descriptions and difficult to identify shapes which are not part of their descriptions.

Method
Ss were shown geometric patterns such as Figure 2.21, followed after a brief interval by a shape. On half the trials, this shape was a component part of the pattern and on half the trials it was not. A pattern repetition counted as a pattern part (see Figure 2.22 for examples). Ss were asked to press one button if the shape was part of the pattern and another button if it was not.

Results

Positive pattern parts		Non-pattern parts	
	Correct responses (out of 80)		Correct responses (out of 80)
	78		
			72
	66		
			68
	63		
			52
	52		
	11		50

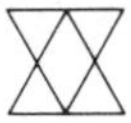

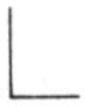

Figure 2.22   Number of correct responses for pattern parts and non-pattern parts

Figure 2.22 shows the total number of correct identifications for each pattern part. A pattern repetition was the easiest to identify correctly. However, this does not mean that Ss were storing the patterns as templates, since among the remaining pattern parts some were much easier to identify than others. This supports the hypothesis that Ss store the presented patterns as pattern parts, together with rules for linking them up (i.e. structural descriptions).

SAQ 20
From the results shown in Figure 2.22, which of the following structural descriptions do you think most Ss were using for Figure 2.21?
(a) A diamond shape with each side forming one side of an equilateral triangle.
(b) A regular parallelogram superimposed with an identical parallelogram such that the long sides of one bisect the long sides of the other, and the short sides of one form a continuous line with the short sides of the others.

Notice that in SAQ 20 the structural descriptions are expressed in words, but given the unwieldy result, it is more than likely that mentally stored structural descriptions are in the form of abstract, non-verbal propositions.

Reed's work is concerned with structural descriptions of two-dimensional patterns. Sutherland (1973) points out that the principle significance of two-dimensional patterns in the real world is that they usually signify three-dimensional objects. For instance, many drawings represent three-dimensional objects and scenes. The retinal image is itself a two-dimensional representation of the three-dimensional world. Could a system of structural descriptions provide the basis for recognizing three-dimensional objects from such two-dimensional patterns?

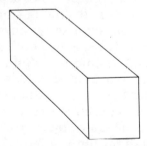

Figure 2.23

Figure 2.23 is a line drawing, and here are three different ways of describing it:
(i) Nine straight lines, joined in a particular way, and including three short horizontals and three short verticals all of the same length, and three long diagonals, all of the same length. (N.B. A proper

119

structural description would specify the rules linking the lines, but these are omitted for brevity.)

(ii)   Three regions, a square and two parallelograms, joined together in a particular way;

(iii)   Two-dimensional representation of a three-dimensional cuboid, having two square surfaces and four rectangular surfaces, of particular sizes.

Each of the three descriptions is valid in a different *domain* (two-dimensional *drawing*; two-dimensional *geometric form*; three-dimensional *object*). However, only one of the three descriptions also applies to Figure 2.24, which we recognize as the same object viewed from a different angle.

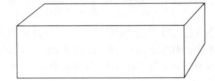

Figure 2.24

SAQ 21
Which of the three descriptions applies to both line drawings?

Why is it just this third description which applies to both drawings? If you look again at the first two descriptions you will note that they are specific to the particular position from which the figure is viewed. Once we look at the same figure from a different angle, they no longer apply. These descriptions are known as *viewer-centred* descriptions. In contrast, the third description does not depend on viewing position. It still applies when we look at the figure from a different angle. This is known as an *object-centred* description.

The fact that we actually recognize both arrangements of lines as the same three-dimensional object led Sutherland (1973) to propose that objects must be represented within memory as structural descriptions of this third kind, i.e. within the object domain. If we did not possess these object-centred structural descriptions, we would be unable to recognize the same object from its many different two-dimensional representations (on the retina, in pictures, etc.).

However, descriptions within the object domain are not enough on their own. The input to the visual system can be thought of as a two-dimensional description in the retinal domain, in the form of a map showing which retinal cells are stimulated and how strongly. As we have seen, the same object or pattern viewed on different occasions can produce an almost infinite number of descriptions within the retinal domain. These are processed into a number of intermediate forms (e.g. features, groupings of features) which can themselves be thought of as descriptions in different domains. Ultimately, however, these descriptions are translated into an object-centred description which enables us to recognize and categorize the objects from which they originate. Sutherland concluded that there must be, stored in memory, descriptions of patterns within many different domains, together with rules for mapping these descriptions onto one another, and onto object-centred descriptions. The real problem for any theory of visual perception is to work out what these descriptions are, and what are the rules for mapping them onto one another.

Summary of Section 6

- A structural description is a set of propositions describing a pattern in terms of those parts which are needed to reconstruct the pattern, plus the rules needed for linking them up.
- A psychological theory of structural descriptions assumes that patterns (including objects) are mentally represented as structural descriptions both for identification and for storage in memory.
- Reed has provided evidence that geometric patterns are mentally represented as structural descriptions.
- Sutherland has argued that the mental representation required to recognize the same object from its varying representations in two-dimensional domains consists of rules which translate structural descriptions in these two-dimensional domains into a structural description in the object domain.

7   The AI approach to vision

Most of our discussion has focused on the operating principles or algorithms by which inputs to the visual system are translated into outputs (what we perceive). To elucidate these operating principles, we have considered how perceptual outputs are influenced by particular types of input, and have attempted to infer what goes on in between. For instance, by studying people's perceptions of simple elements arranged in particular ways, we have inferred that the visual system groups inputs according to similarity, proximity, continuity, etc. By studying the 'mistakes' made by the visual system in interpreting certain arrangements of lines, we have inferred that visual perception is itself a process of inference.

There is, however, a rather different way of trying to find out how visual perception works. Instead of trying to infer the workings of an existing system, one can set out to build an *artificial vision system* from scratch. This is an extremely difficult enterprise and invariably only partially successful, if measured against the elegant complexity of living visual systems. However, it has the advantage that any system which is constructed is necessarily fully understood by the person who has built it. For this reason, the study of artificial vision systems has contributed a good deal to our understanding of vision in living organisms (*biological vision*). On the other hand, artificial vision systems do not all have the same objective of 'simulating' biological vision so the relationship between artificial and biological systems is a complex one.

7.1   The objectives of artificial vision systems

The researcher who sets out to build an artificial vision system is not *necessarily* aiming to create a model of human vision; he or she may be aiming to produce a device that can perform a rather specific visual function (for example, a robot in a car factory that can identify objects on the assembly line; or in medical diagnosis, a computer that can 'see' defective cells in a blood sample). Alternatively the researcher's aim may be to construct and test a general theory of vision, the principles of which will apply to any visual system whether biological or artificial. This latter enterprise is often known as *image understanding*. Of course, many researchers are interested in both theoretical implications and practical applications.

The designer of the artificial system *may* draw on what is known about biological vision and incorporate some of the same operating principles in his or her system. On the other hand, he or she may choose to incorporate different operating principles (or algorithms) in the computer program which implements the visual task. Since, in any case, there are huge gaps in our knowledge of how biological vision works, the designer cannot *copy* the biological system, but must *create* a solution to a 'visual problem'.

The extent to which artificial and biological systems do resemble each other is considerably influenced by the constraints to which they are subject. Any vision system designed to operate in the real world is subject to certain general constraints imposed by the nature of the real world and the need to divide it into meaningful 'chunks'. Objects in the real world obey certain laws (e.g. an object can only be in one place at a time; one solid object in front of another partly conceals it). The need to distinguish between objects of different shapes or of different sizes, or to recognize the equivalence of different viewpoints of the same scene, are basic if a system is to function successfully. In so far as they are subject to these same general constraints, artificial and biological systems are likely to have things in common.

On the other hand, to the extent that different vision systems are designed for different purposes, the constraints upon them will differ. Humans do not normally need to see under water so the design of their visual system is not constrained by the need to interpret patterns of light refracted by water. The visual system of a fish, or of a robot used to spot patches of rust on the underwater legs of an oil rig, must work within these constraints. It is clearly important to specify the general and specific constraints to which a particular system is subject, if we are to understand the system and compare it with other systems. This is closely related to David Marr's claim that one must specify the *computational theory* of a system in order to understand how it works (see Section 2.1)

What kind of constraints are imposed by the nature of the raw material from which a system is constructed? It is often suggested that it is in principle possible for different kinds of hardware to achieve the same functions. This is certainly true for artificial vision systems, which means that the constraints imposed by computer hardware alone are not very great. The hardware of biological vision systems is considerably more specialized. Complex functions, tailored to the individual needs of particular organisms, are achieved at the expense of flexibility in the alternative functions which any one biological system can achieve. Insects, but not humans, can see ultra-violet light. Frogs will snap up prey which moves in front of their eyes, but will starve to death if the prey does not move. These are the sorts of constraints imposed by the specific hardware of biological vision systems.

Differences in the functions of, and constraints upon, artificial and biological vision systems may affect one's criterion of whether they 'work'. Suppose we were trying to program a computer to 'see' a chair in a room. How would we decide whether the computer had 'seen' the chair? We know whether a person can see the chair because she can say what she is seeing or provide a written description of it. She can also answer questions such as 'Is what you see a chair or a table?' She can sit down on the chair, walk around it, or push it up to a table. We can use all of these 'outputs' as criteria of seeing. The criteria of computer vision are often more limited than this. A system may be said to 'see' if it can produce a description of an object, but this does not necessarily mean it can walk round the object or use it appropriately. To conclude, if an artificial vision system works successfully, we cannot necessarily infer that this is how human vision works. We can, at best, only conclude that this is one of the ways it could work.

7.2   The world of toy blocks: Roberts' program

Our discussion implies that one of the main decisions to be taken when designing an AI vision system is the scope of functions it should perform. As we have seen, the human visual system is capable of a wide range of complex achievements. Should the scope of an artificial system be comparably broad? Or should it aim to tackle a relatively specific visual problem in the hope that the principles developed will generalize to other tasks.

Recent work by David Marr and others has adopted the first strategy. He has aimed to design a fairly comprehensive visual system in the light of a proper computational theory which specifies what general functions perception must achieve. Earlier work, to be discussed in this section, adopted the second strategy, confining itself to the somewhat restricted and unnatural problem of recognizing *toy blocks*, and concentrating on the algorithms required to achieve this.

The goal was to program a computer to analyse a scene composed of a heap of toy blocks like the one in Figure 2.25.

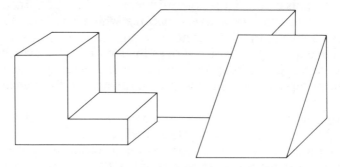

Figure 2.25   A 'blocks world' scene (from Boden, 1977)

The computer is supposed to analyse the scene in such a way that it can identify the constituent blocks. The *input* to the system is either a TV image of the scene, a photograph, or a line drawing.

Typically the *output* of such a system is a description of the sizes and shapes of the blocks in the scene, or a diagram of the same scene from a different viewpoint. In attempting to interpret the input data, toy blocks programs rely to a considerable extent on different kinds of knowledge. Some of this is specific knowledge about the shapes of the different kinds of blocks. The remainder is general knowledge about the laws of perspective and the projection rules by which three-dimensional shapes can be derived from two-dimensional representations such as line drawings, photographs or TV images.

One of the first of the blocks world programs was written by Roberts (1965). It accepted as input photographs of scenes consisting of three kinds of blocks: cubes, wedges and hexagonal cylinders, as shown in Figure 2.26.

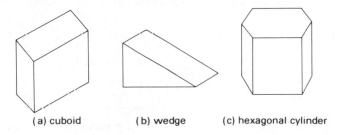

(a) cuboid   (b) wedge   (c) hexagonal cylinder

Figure 2.26   The three kinds of object recognized by Roberts' program (from Boden, 1977)

Roberts' program contained stored 'models' of each of these types of block, and looked for 'evidence' to show which ones were present. To do this it employed the following operations, in which top-down processing (exploiting stored knowledge) heavily influences the bottom-up analysis of cues:
(a) Find a cue
(b) Select a hypothesis to make sense of the cue
(c) Draw inferences about what other cues should be present
(d) Check for presence of these cues
(e) Confirm or discard the hypothesis
These operations were applied at two distinct stages in the program. In the first stage, known as the *line finder stage*, the program constructed a line drawing of the toy blocks scene. To do this the input photograph was first converted into a 'digitized' array of 256×256 picture points. Each of these picture points represents the brightness value of a specific location in the input picture, and is known as a *pixel* (picture element). The way in which the brightness varies across the array provides cues which the program interprets, drawing on stored knowledge about how shadows and bright areas relate to edges and how changes of brightness indicate surface boundaries.

The second stage of Roberts' program was the *picture interpreter stage* which interpreted the lines in terms of 3D objects. To do this the program utilized its stored models of the three types of blocks. These were much like structural descriptions, though Roberts referred to them as *prototypes*. The program started by identifying cues for these prototypes from the line drawing produced by the line finder stage. These cues consisted of two-dimensional shapes which were consistent with one or other of the three block prototypes. For instance, a triangular shape is a cue for the wedge prototype because it is a component part of this block (see Figure 2.26b).

SAQ 22
For which of the three blocks do the following shapes act as cues?
>   Square
>   Triangle

The program adopted as its hypothesis the prototype to which these configuration cues pointed and then compared this prototype with further configuration cues. In the course of this matching, the prototype might be 'stretched' or 'rotated' to allow for variations in the size or orientation of the blocks being identified. If there was a good enough match between the configuration cues and this prototype, the hypothesis was confirmed and the block identified as a cube, wedge, or cylinder. If the match was poor, different cues would be selected and the remaining prototypes considered. In the final output, the program would identify blocks whether they were separate, as shown in Figure 2.26, or superimposed, in each case specifying their size and relative position. In addition, the program could produce alternative views of the scene, using stored knowledge of the laws of geometry.

SAQ 23
Is the final output of Roberts' program an object-centred or viewer-centred representation? (Refer back to Section 6 if you are unsure.)

7.3   Guzman's program

Guzman's (1969) SEE program was designed, not to identify different types of block, but to discover how many separate blocks were present in a scene where the blocks were jumbled together, overlapping and partly obscuring each other. To do this, the program needed to define object boundaries so as to distinguish or *segregate* the pile of blocks from its background, and to work out where one block ended and another block began. Unlike Roberts' program, Guzman's program did not rely on stored models to guide the selection of cues to fit a particular interpretation. Instead it drew conclusions about which regions of the input were linked, using the cues provided by different kinds of line junction and interpreting them according to set rules. For example, the rule applying to *arrow junctions* (Figure 27a) is that the two regions divided by the shaft of the arrow are both surfaces of the same object. The rule for *fork junctions* (Figure 27b) is that all three regions meeting at the fork are related. In contrast, the rule for *T junctions* (Figure 27c) is that region C is not usually joined to A or B. Some regions would be found to have two or more line junctions linking them and these would be grouped together, on the principle that the more links there are between regions, the more likely they are to belong to the same object.

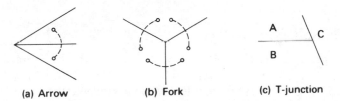

(a) Arrow   (b) Fork   (c) T-junction

Figure 2.27   Junction cues used by Guzman's program

SAQ 24
Do you think this program works bottom-up or top down?

The interest of this program is that it shows how grouping rules (cf. Section 4) can be used to derive three-dimensional objects from a two-dimensional input. However, junction cues are often ambiguous or misleading. For instance in Figure 2.28, the junction at A is

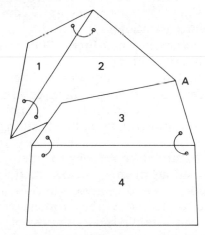

Figure 2.28   A pseudo-arrow junction at A. Regions 2 and 3 do not belong to the same object (from Boden, 1977).

127

somewhat like an arrow junction, but it does *not* signify two adjacent regions of the same object. Guzman tackled this problem in an *ad hoc* fashion, adding additional link-inhibiting rules to prevent the program making mistakes. However, these additional rules were not based on general geometrical constraints but more specific trial-and-error solutions to specific types of ambiguity. With each additional rule, the number of possible 'interpretations' for a given set of cues multiplied until there were too many alternatives for even a large computer program to explore and assess. This problem is known as the *combinatorial explosion*.

7.4   *Waltz's program*

Waltz's program (1975) attempted to deal with this combinatorial explosion, developing ideas that Huffman (1971) and Clowes (1971) also incorporated in programs. He made much more use of knowledge about the geometry of solid bodies than Guzman did. This meant that the conclusions drawn from particular types of cue could be guided by stored knowledge about what sorts of block scenarios are possible in the real world. Thus the program did not generate quite such a multiplicity of interpretations for a given input.

An important stage in the program consisted of labelling each of the edges in a toy blocks scene as concave (pointing away from the viewer), convex (pointing towards the viewer) or occluding (signifying a boundary between two solids). To do this the program drew upon stored knowledge to guide its interpretations of junction cues in the scene. As Figure 29a shows, an arrow junction is consistent with three physically different interpretations.

Similarly, the *L*-junction shown in Figure 20b is consistent with six physically different interpretations.

The program stored all the physically possible interpretations of such junction cues in the form of a *junction dictionary*. Figure 29c shows an arrangement of toy blocks with an *L*-junction at A and an arrow junction at B. Given the numerous possible labellings of the line AB which could be derived from the junction dictionary, the program drew upon a further type of stored knowledge to rule out any physically incompatible interpretations of this pair of junctions. For instance, as there is an *L*-junction at A and an arrow junction at B, the junction dictionary might lead to the line AB being interpreted as concave at A and convex at B. But it is physically impossible for a line to be concave at one end and convex at the other. This type of knowledge was incorporated in *filtering algorithms*. In this way, the program

Figure 2.29a   The three physically possible interpretations of an arrow junction. A minus signifies a concave edge; a plus signifies a convex edge; an arrow on the line signifies an occluding edge (nearest surface to right of arrow)

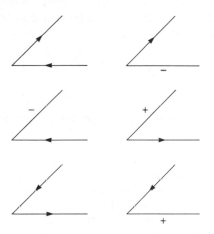

Figure 2.29b   The six physically possible interpretations of an *L*-junction

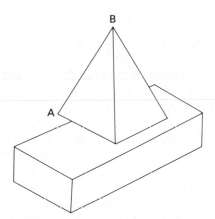

Figure 2.29c

limited the possible interpretations of the scene to a more manageable number.

Another strategy for limiting the combinatorial explosion was to label the scene components starting at the outer edges of the scene and working towards the centre. There are fewer possible interpretations for lines at the boundary between scene and background so once the outer links are labelled, the number of possible labellings for the central part of the scene is reduced.

Waltz's program also utilized cues provided by shadows. It was able to output a 3D description of objects in a shadowy scene; missing or obscured lines could be inferred; and the program could also perform the difficult task of recognizing the equivalence of different views of the same scene. Nevertheless, its performance was far from perfect. It still made mistakes, and could be 'fooled' into identifying 'objects' even if these could not exist in the real world. Even with the additional stored knowledge at its disposal, it would not resolve all of the ambiguities among the cues in its input.

7.5   *Limitations of the blocks world approach*

Each of the programs designed to analyse blocks world scenes is an attempt to overcome the limitations of an earlier program. The more successful programs have worked only because they have incorporated domain-specific knowledge about toy blocks in the program, either in the form of specific models like Roberts' prototype, or of more general geometric assumptions like Waltz's junction dictionary and filtering algorithms.

The main interest of blocks world programs is that they aim to recover a 3D description from a 2D line drawing. Since the human visual system performs a similar function in extracting a 3D representation from the 2D retinal image, it could be argued that these programs achieve greater ecological validity than experimental studies employing simple 2D patterns. Yet it is clear that even if the human perceiver uses *some* of the same cues and operations as the programs, many of the operating principles must be very different. Human perceivers do not seem to conduct a search through umpteen possible interpretations of a scene. They seem able to extract a single interpretation in a way that is natural, obvious and instantaneous. For human perceivers, object recognition is not confined to the simplified shapes of the toy blocks world, but copes easily with an unlimited range of real world objects. Objects like a face, a potato or a leaf are very variable, are not subject to geometrical constraints and may lack defining features. Since the human vision system can assign such objects to appropriate categories with little difficulty, its operating principles cannot resemble those of the artificial systems described above at all closely.

One reason why the scene analysis programs were relatively limited, laborious and fallible is that they relied upon the very restricted range of cues provided by lines, junctions, etc. Powerful cues provided by texture, movement and stereoscopic disparity were not exploited. The more recent computational approaches to vision, described in Part III, are designed to utilize a much richer range and variety of information from the visual input. They therefore provide a fairer test of what can be achieved by bottom-up processing of the input without the influence of specific knowledge working in a top-down direction.

Summary of Section 7

- The attempt to design an artificial vision system provides an alternative strategy for understanding visual perception, but insights into human perception are usually indirect.
- An early blocks world program developed by Roberts aimed to identify the types of blocks present in a scene, using stored knowledge of blocks to interpret cues.
- An alternative approach by Guzman used set rules rather than stored knowledge of blocks to draw conclusions about different kinds of line junctions.
- Waltz's program attempted to limit the combinatorial explosion by using knowledge of the geometry of solids to limit the conclusions drawn from cues.
- The limitations of toy blocks programs point to the need to exploit more powerful and complex cues in the visual input.

Further reading

1 Marr, D. 'Vision: the philosophy and the approach' in Aitkenhead and Slack (eds) (1985). A brief introduction to Marr's ideas, including his philosophy of 'levels'; adapted from the first chapter of his book *Vision* (1982).

2 Bruce, V. and Green, P. (1985) *Visual Perception: Physiology, Psychology and Ecology*. An excellent and detailed coverage of a wide range of topics.

3 Pomerantz, J. R. 'Perceptual organization in information processing' in Aitkenhead and Slack (eds) (1985). A review of modern experimental work on perceptual organization and global processing phenomena.

4 Gregory, R. L. and Gombrich, E. G. (1973) *Illusion in Nature and Art*. An entertaining book bringing together artistic and scientific aspects of illusion. Includes a good statement of Gregory's theory and

a discussion by Blakemore of how the 'hardware' of the visual system can produce illusions.

5 Gibson, J. J. (1979) *The Ecological Approach to Visual Perception.* Gibson's intriguing account of his theory.

6 Boden, M. (1977) *Artificial Intelligence and Natural Man.* Includes a good discussion of toy blocks programs.

Part III
The Computational
Approach to Vision

John P. Frisby

Contents

1   *The vision problem*

Imagine you were trying to design a robot capable of playing the young child's game of building castles out of a heap of blocks like those shown in Figure 3.1; or, perhaps more plausibly, assembling the blocks as part of an industrial assembly process. You would have to start by equipping the robot with some means of looking at the blocks to find out where they are, what their shapes are, and so on. How would you go about designing a visual system that could match the visual capabilities of a human being for seeing what needs to be done to construct a tower?

Figure 3.1   A scene made up of the three blocks awaiting industrial assembly: Block A fits on to the peg of Block B, the two of them then to be capped by Block C

The first thing you might do would be to equip the robot with an optical device of some sort, perhaps a TV camera, that could capture one or more images of the scene. That would be a sensible start as we know that human eyes are optical devices and they set going the whole business of human vision. So having done this, you would have arranged for the robot to receive as its visual input light images of the scene. But what would you do next?

In thinking about this 'vision problem' you would soon come to the conclusion that the images would have to be analysed or interpreted in some way in order to obtain useful information about the scene. For example, the robot would need to discover from the images how far away the blocks are so that it could send information to its arm control mechanisms about the reaching distance required. Also, the robot would need to discover something about the shape of the blocks, so that the arm could be directed to grasp them in appropriate places and to stack them one on top of another in a sensible way.

All this information is so readily given to us by our own visual system that it is natural to think it must be a simple matter to enable a robot to extract such information from its input images. Indeed, most people take vision so much for granted that they take some time to realize that there is a problem at all. 'Surely having an input image *is* the same as "seeing" a scene?' is quite often the reaction of a newcomer to the field. The answer is 'Not at all!', as anyone knows only too well who has actually tried to build an artificial visual system capable of using images to guide a task such as stacking blocks one on top of another. Don't be misled by looking at Figure 3.1 and thinking that just because you as a human can so easily see so many attributes of the blocks scene that it is equally easy to get a computer to do likewise. It isn't! By the end of this Part you should be able to appreciate some of the difficulties.

To state the *vision problem* succinctly, we can say that it amounts to finding out how to extract useful information about a scene from images of that scene. By 'useful information' is meant information about the scene in a form which is suitable for guiding the thoughts and actions of the total system of which the vision system is a part. Hence vision is sometimes described as the business of making *explicit* information about the scene that is only *implicit* in the original image. This *implicit/explicit distinction* will be illustrated many times in the following discussion. The basic idea is however quite simple: useful information about the world 'out there' needs to be computed from visual images in a usable form, i.e. 'made explicit'. Prior to visual analysis, this information is not available in a form that can be used because it is 'only implicit' in the input images. The aim of the *computational approach* to vision is to specify the computations necessary to extract useful scene information from images.

Another way of expressing the same basic notion is to say that vision achieves *inverse projection*. Optical devices, such as cameras or human eyeballs, project an image of a scene: it is the task of a visual system connected to such a device (i.e. a visual 'brain') to work the other way around—i.e. inversely—and build up a description of the scene which produced the image in the first place. It is for this reason that this general approach to vision is often known as *Image Understanding (IU)*.

The overall goal of Part III of this volume is to illustrate some of the difficulties that are encountered in trying to solve the vision problem. The linking theme will be a particular approach to the problem that was pioneered by the late David Marr, beginning in the mid-1970s.

1.1   The influence of Marr

Marr was a mathematician who always planned to study the brain once he had completed the basic mathematical training that he thought essential for that task. He began with an investigation of the computations being performed by the elaborate neural architecture of the cerebellum, a large structure located at the rear of the brain long known to be involved in motor control. He became dissatisfied with speculating about neural structures *per se* and decided that what was missing was an analysis of the functions they perform. That led him to move from Cambridge, England, to Massachussetts Institute of Technology in Cambridge, New England, to learn about Artificial Intelligence. There he became deeply interested in vision, influenced in no small measure by the work of Horn, Land, and their collaborators.

Marr combined a remarkable ability for selecting 'good problems' (that is, tractable, timely, but non-trivial problems) with superb flair for integrating computational, neurophysiological and psychophysical knowledge in tackling them. It is probably true to say that his death from leukaemia at the age of thirty-five at the height of his powers robbed him of any chance of contributing a fundamentally important 'enduring result' to visual science, the equivalent of the double helix idea of DNA structure, or a deep mathematical theorem capable of standing the test of time. It is, in my view, unlikely that any one of his papers will be read as a classic in decades ahead for the specific visual theories it contains. Instead, Marr's lasting influence will probably be the way he has brought a deeper realization to those investigating biological visual systems of the need to study, not just the phenomena of biological vision, nor just the neural mechanisms that might underlie them, but, at least as important, the nature of the visual task being solved by those visual systems.

1.2   Vision as a sequence of representations

> . . . vision is considered to be a sequence of processes that are successively extracting visual information from one representation, organizing it, and making it explicit in another representation to be used by other processes. Viewed in this way it is conceptually convenient to treat vision as computationally *modular* and *sequential*. This is not to deny that future implementations of competent visual systems will find it advantageous to utilize modules that are operating in parallel and that complex control structures managing their interactions might be necessary, both within and between levels in a processing hierarchy. It is, however, to suggest that at present it seems best to direct attention to understanding the principles that can underlie the design of modules that are capable of extracting useful information from a particular type of visual information.   (Mayhew and Frisby, 1984)

The above summarizes some important aspects of Marr's approach, notably that visual analysis is best carried out by a series of computations within the total visual system, each one performed as far as possible by an independent vision module. Each module is specified in terms of its input representation, output representation, and a method for solving the computational problems of getting from input to output. Various examples of vision modules will be described here, each one under the following headings.

1 *Input representation:* the information made explicit by the preceding stage of analysis.
2 *Output representation:* the information made explicit by the current processing stage.

Both input and output representations are expressed in terms of elementary units called *primitives*.

3 *The computational problem:* what needs to be computed in order to get from input to output? Usually this means stating a goal very clearly, being explicit about the nature of an ambiguity to be resolved, or the exact nature of a compromise that must be found between competing goals.
4 *The computational theory:* the job of the computational theory is to provide a well-founded method for solving the computational problem using knowledge derived from the nature of the task and/or the nature of the world being viewed.

Different modules can be grouped into three broad classes according to the types of representations they compute—image descriptions, scene surface descriptions, and 3D object model descriptions. Figure 3.2 illustrates how Marr saw the various types forming a sequence of three broadly distinct stages of visual analysis. This framework is also summarized in the chart on page 177.

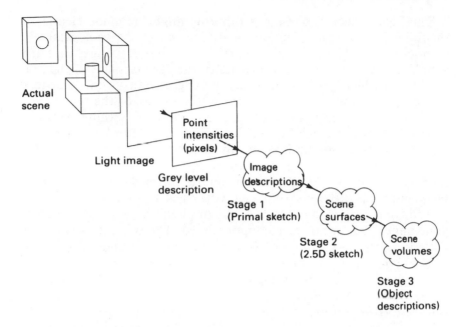

Figure 3.2   Marr's three major stages of representation: descriptions of image intensity changes (primal sketch); descriptions of surfaces in depth (2.5D sketch); descriptions of volumes (3D object models)

It is important to recognize that the above scheme for studying vision makes no mention of the physical structures, such as parts of the human brain or the components of a computer, that might actually carry out the tasks of any given module. Those structures are often referred to as the *hardware*. If we want to understand any particular visual system completely, be it man-made or biological, then finding out how its hardware implements a given computational theory is essential, as well as being of great interest. But the central tenet of Marr's approach is that studying the hardware is in itself not enough. To do that is to neglect the crucially important requirement of understanding the nature of the task that the hardware is carrying out. Emphasis on devising well-founded methods for solving visual processing tasks irrespective of the design of any particular hardware for implementing those methods is *the* salient feature of Marr's approach. He argued that, without this topmost level of analysis (which he called the *computational theory* level, and which he believed had been largely neglected by neurophysiologists and psychophysicists), we will never have a deep understanding of the phenomena and mechanisms of biological vision systems—we will never know *why* the hardware they possess is designed the way it is.

This central aspect of Marr's thinking might be made clearer by the following example. Suppose you discovered an archaeological relic composed of various pieces of clockwork gearing. It would be a fairly simple task to describe the properties of the various parts of the relic in terms of which gear turned which, what gear ratios were embedded in the system, and so on. But your understanding of the relic would not be complete until you knew the function of the 'thing' you had discovered. Is it a clock? Or could it be a calculator of some sort? Or the control mechanism of an industrial device? Once that information was available, your appreciation of the logic underlying the relic's design would be dramatically transformed—indeed it would be qualitatively different from what you knew at first, and would lead you to appreciate many aspects of the mechanism which had hitherto gone unnoticed, or any rate unappreciated. The point here is that to understand the device fully you would need to know about the structure of the task which it was designed to solve, as well as the structure of the mechanism itself. The same seems to be true of visual mechanisms discovered by neurophysiologists: the properties of neurones can now be described in considerable detail, but to understand their design fully needs a deep understanding of the tasks they are performing.

For complex information processing systems, it is often helpful to distinguish another level of analysis lying in between those of computational theory and hardware. This is the *algorithm* level. An algorithm is a set of procedures which specify in detail a sequence of operations that achieve a given end. Consider, for example, trying to understand a programmable calculator set up to perform some statistical computation, say, work out a standard deviation. The computational theory level of understanding would be the logic underlying the use of the standard deviation as a measure of variance—its statistical properties, the assumptions required for its proper use, etc. Those considerations are rather far removed from the business of actually calculating a standard deviation in a convenient and speedy manner. A standard deviation calculation can be done in a variety of ways, each more or less suitable to a given application. For example, some procedures for calculating the standard deviation take advantage of arithmetical short-cuts that considerably reduce the number of operations required.

In short, different ways (i.e. different 'algorithms') for doing the calculation exist, each one involving a different set of detailed procedures—but all computing the same standard deviation and each therefore having the same ultimate statistical significance (i.e. the same 'computational theory'). Choosing a particular algorithm will depend upon such matters as the form in which the data exists and the nature of the hardware that is to implement the algorithm. As an example of the latter kind of consideration, if the calculator had a rather limited memory it might prove necessary to avoid using an algorithm needing all the original data to be stored at any one time. Here is a case of a choice of algorithm being influenced strongly by a hardware limitation — while at the same time showing how the algorithm level is separate from wholly hardware matters, such as issues to do with memory circuit design, cooling, power supplies, etc.

The point of this example is to illustrate Marr's contention that in trying to understand an information processing device — here a programmed calculator capable of computing a standard deviation — it is necessary to keep clearly distinct the issues to be faced at three different levels: computational theory, algorithm, and hardware. These levels need to be carefully distinguished while at the same time recognizing that they are complementary. Each one has its own preoccupations and concerns but all are important for a full understanding of what is going on.

Marr's claim is that many investigations of biological vision systems, and the creation of many man-made ones, have failed to recognize the importance of these level-of-analysis distinctions, with the result that progress has been slowed (Marr, 1982). In what follows, emphasis will be given to the computational theory level but some reference will also be made to algorithm and hardware matters.

Summary of Section 1

- The 'vision problem' can be defined as finding ways of extracting useful information about a scene from an input image of the scene.
- Vision, according to the approach of Marr, is to be conceived of as requiring a sequence of representations, each one derived from predecessors by an appropriate set of processes.
- The sequence of representations can be grouped under three heads according to the nature of the descriptions that they deal with; image descriptions (Primal Sketch), scene surface descriptions (2.5D Sketch), and volume descriptions (3D Object Models).
- Each representation can be thought of as being delivered by a 'vision module' specified in terms of its input representation (the starting information), an output representation (the derived information which acts as input for another module), and the solution to one or more computational problems (description of a method for deriving the output representation from the input representation).
- Complex information processing systems need to be analysed at three distinct but complementary levels. The computational theory

141

level is concerned with understanding the nature of the computational task and in establishing a computational theory capable of solving the problems presented by that task. The algorithm level is concerned with specifying in detail a sequence of operations to get from input to output representation using the principles set out by the computational theory. The hardware level is concerned with the design of a set of physical structures appropriate for implementing the algorithm.

● The computational approach to vision attempts to find methods for solving the collection of information processing problems that together constitute the vision problem.

2   Stage 1: Computing image descriptions—the primal sketch

This stage is concerned with deriving *two-dimensional (2D)* descriptions of significant *light intensity changes* in the input image. The sub-stages in this process are shown in Figure 3.3.

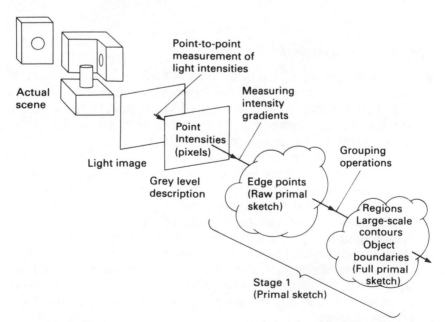

Figure 3.3   Stage 1: Computing the primal sketch—light image; grey level description; raw primal sketch; full primal sketch

2.1   Generating a grey level description from the light image

Returning to the problem posed in Section 1, how can we start the business of getting some useful information from the pattern of light that constitutes the input image captured by our optical device? It turns out that both biological and man-made vision systems find it convenient to begin this process by measuring the intensity of light at every 'point' in the incoming light image. And in a colour vision system, the intensity of different wavelengths at each point would be measured too. For the purposes of this account, however, we will simplify matters by considering only monochromatic images, and only static ones at that (i.e. single snap-shots rather than sequences of images capturing object movements).

The input is then the pattern of light that constitutes the light image. The optical device focuses this on to a light-sensitive surface of some kind which is capable of measuring light intensities at every point. For a computer vision system, these light intensities are represented by a 2D array of numbers that describe the image intensities point by point (see Figure 3.4). The numbers in this array are called *pixels* (short for *picture elements*). The whole array is called a *grey level description*, for the simple reason that, for monochromatic images, the pixel numbers code the intensity of light at each point on a grey

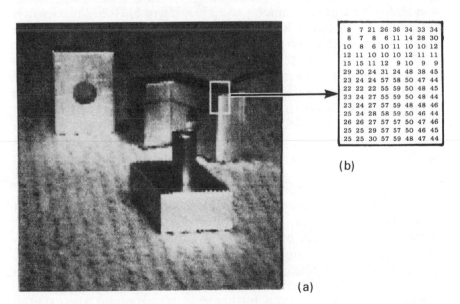

(b)

(a)

Figure 3.4   Grey level description: (a) image of blocks scene; (b) pixels comprising a small insert of (a)—high pixel numbers represent brightest areas in image

scale running from black through greys to white. The variations in intensity relate to the amount of light reflected by or emitted by the surfaces of objects present in the scene.

You should beware of falling into the trap of thinking that, because your own visual system so effortlessly 'sees' characteristics of the scene shown in Figure 3.4, that the array of pixels amounts to the same thing as human visual perceptions. The pixels code only *local intensity values*; all else is left implicit. It is the task of subsequent stages of visual analysis to extract scene information, using the pixels as its initial database.

The density of pixels can be varied to suit the needs of the visual system being built. If there are not many pixels, so that each pixel has to represent light intensities averaged over a substantial area of the image, then the resulting pixel array will have a correspondingly *coarse resolution*. Carried to extremes, this can produce block pictures of the kind sometimes used in advertisements, where the boundaries between pixels are easily visible to the human eye. On the other hand, if many pixels are used, then the visual system in question will have the information required for *high resolution*, fine detail discriminations. The whole grey level description of the scene in Figure 3.4 (a) is made up of an array of 128×128 pixels. This is adequate for many purposes but is rather coarse by today's computer vision standards which more commonly use 256×256 or 512×512 pixel arrays (an ordinary domestic UK television receiver creates pictures using an array of 625×625 pixels).

The problems to be solved in getting a good grey level description are largely optical, photochemical, and/or electrical in nature and will not be pursued here. Suffice it to say that the 2D array of pixels shown in Figure 3.4(b) seems to have its equivalent in the 2D array of *receptors* (rods and cones) which constitute the *retina*, i.e. the receptor cells at the back of the human eyeball. The polarization level of each receptor cell (the voltage difference across its membrane) probably serves much the same role in recording light intensities as each number in the grey level description of a computer system.

By way of a reminder about the route we are trying to follow, it is worth emphasizing that an array of pixels is a representation making explicit only very local point-by-point variations in light intensities. Everything else is left implicit. It is the task of a visual system to move from this initial 'pointillist' pixel representation of its input light image to other representations conveying a rich description of the scene — representations making explicit what objects are present, their spatial layout, and the illumination, orientation, texture, reflectance, range and movement of their surfaces.

2.2   Computing the raw primal sketch

Having obtained an array of pixels, the customary next step is to compute a description of the *intensity changes* that exist all over the image. To grasp what this means, it is helpful to think of the numbers in the array of pixels as giving land heights all over a hilly terrain, with the higher pixel numbers representing 'hills' of bright regions and lower pixel numbers the 'valleys' of darker areas in the image. Computing a description of intensity changes then amounts to mapping the slopes and valleys of the terrain, the mountains and ridges. In terms of the things to be found in images, this amounts to computing descriptions of *edges* from light intensity changes arising at the boundaries of objects, surface texture markings and shadows. The value of the hilly terrain metaphor is that it gives an insight into why this problem is one of measuring intensity changes, technically often referred to as 'measuring intensity gradients', from the numbers comprising the 2D array of pixels.

A rich description of image intensity changes was called by Marr the *primal sketch*: 'primal' because he regarded it as the database for all subsequent visual processing and 'sketch' because it is *viewpoint-dependent*. That is, a different edge representation (a different primal sketch) would be found if the viewer were to look at the scene from a different position and so receive from it a different image. Marr also distinguished between the very first stages of this representation, which he called the 'raw' primal sketch, and later stages, called the 'full' primal sketch. Using our scheme for setting out each module, we have the following for the raw primal sketch.

Input representation   The grey level description, that is, a 2D array of pixels making explicit local pointillist image intensities.

Output representation   The raw primal sketch showing the locations of primitives, called here *edge points*, that represent intensity changes found in the image. The position of each edge point is given in *X and Y image coordinates*, and is also described in terms of other *parameters* giving its contrast, orientation, and scale (steep or shallow intensity change). Other raw primal sketch primitives are small blobs, edge segments, and terminations of edge segments.

Figure 3.5 shows a picture of the kind of representation that we are after as far as edge points are concerned. Each dot in the picture reflects the fact that the computer has found an edge point at the location shown. This is often described as the computer making an *assertion* of an edge point's existence. In the computer's memory will

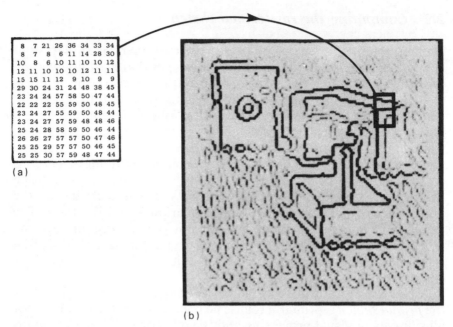

8	7	21	26	36	34	33	34
8	7	8	6	11	14	28	30
10	8	6	10	11	10	10	12
12	11	10	10	10	12	11	11
15	15	11	12	9	10	9	9
29	30	24	31	24	48	38	45
23	24	24	57	58	50	47	44
22	22	22	55	59	50	48	45
23	24	27	55	59	50	48	44
23	24	27	57	59	48	48	46
25	24	28	58	59	50	46	44
26	26	27	57	57	50	47	46
25	25	29	57	57	50	46	45
25	25	30	57	59	48	47	44

(a)

(b)

Figure 3.5   From the image intensities represented as pixels in (a), intensity changes are computed to obtain the edge points of the raw primal sketch shown in (b)

be stored the various parameters for each edge point. Figure 3.5 is pointillist in the sense that each edge point is stored independently of the rest, just as each pixel was stored independently of all others in the grey level description. In other words, these edge points have still to be grouped up with their neighbours to derive assertions of blobs, edge segments, etc. Moreover, further grouping still is required to assert the larger scale geometrical distribution and organization of these raw primal sketch primitives necessary for describing, say, the object boundaries of the various blocks. Those larger scale groupings lie in the domain of the full primal sketch. Once again, because your visual system so readily groups these points up into larger structures, don't be misled into thinking that the computer has done so in arriving at Figure 3.5—that comes at the next processing stage. The low level point-by-point property of the edge points in Figure 3.5 is why Marr called this level of representation the raw primal sketch.

The computational problem   Marr and Hildreth (1980) posed the edge point detection problem in the following way. Edge point assertions need to be accurately located (correct X, Y coordinates) and their *scale* (i.e. the *slope*, or *gradient* of intensity changes) also needs to be accurately designated. Now it turns out that these twin requirements are opposing and a way must be found of balancing them; technically, this problem can be stated as asking 'Is there a way of specifying an optimal trade-off between the two requirements of accurate measurements of the location and of the gradient of intensity changes?'

The computational theory   Marr and Hildreth (1980) provide an elegant, though controversial, theory of the edge point detection problem just posed, but it is too technically involved to explain in this elementary introduction to computer vision. Nevertheless, its main outcome is a fascinating one for those interested in natural vision, because it turns out that neural units of the kind found in the early stages of many biological visual systems seem to have just the receptive field properties that the theory demands. That is, these units seem to be hardware designed to implement the theory.

Briefly the *receptive field* of a visual cell (*neurone*) in the eye or brain is defined in terms of the patch of light on the retina that activates it. An important class of retinal ganglion cells have their receptive fields divided into *antagonistic centres and surrounds*. For example, stimulation of the centre of the receptive field of a particular cell will 'excite' the cell to 'fire' (i.e. send information further up the visual system), whereas stimulation of the outer parts of the receptive field will inhibit the cell from firing. Other cells are inhibited by stimulation in the centre and activated by the surrounding area. As a result, for each cell the light falling on different parts of the receptive field is weighted differently in terms of its effect upon the activity of the cell.

Figure 3.6 portrays the *Mexican Hat profile* of *excitation* and *inhibition* for a neurone which is excited by stimulation of its centre and inhibited by stimulation of its surround. Light excites the cell most strongly in the centre of the receptive field, as shown by the height at the 'top' of the hat. Moving out from the centre, the level of excitation falls off quite steeply until at a certain distance from the centre light starts inhibiting activation (the 'brim' of the hat). Such a cell will respond to an edge if the bright side (i.e. high light intensity) of the edge excites the centre of the field and the dimmer side (low light intensity) falls on some part of the inhibitory surround, because then the excitation will exceed the inhibition.

If Marr and Hildreth are right, biological hardware of this general type is implementing a pretty good theory of edge point detection by satisfying the equally desirable but opposing requirements of finding the location of edge points in the image accurately while at the same time giving a good measure of the slopes of intensity change.

We will not go further into the details of the Marr/Hildreth theory, which would require amongst other things explaining how Mexican Hat receptive fields of various sizes are needed to arrive at really

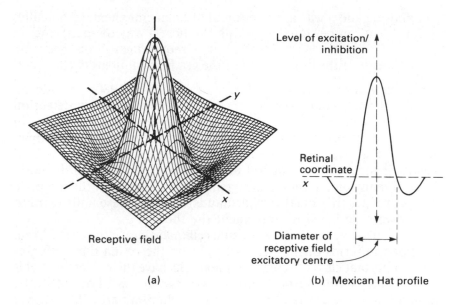

Receptive field   (a)

Level of excitation/ inhibition

Retinal coordinate x

Diameter of receptive field excitatory centre

(b) Mexican Hat profile

Figure 3.6   Mexican Hat pattern of excitation and inhibition of the receptive field of a single visual neurone. A spot of light falling on the centre of the field would cause a high level of excitation; if the spot were then moved to the periphery, the excitation would reduce until in the surround the light would inhibit the cell

satisfactory edge point descriptions. The point of including a brief mention of the theory is to give an example of the central claim made by Marr about understanding biological hardware. In order to understand the nature of the hardware it is necessary to set its properties within a theoretical context which explains why they are the way they are. Merely describing the Mexican Hat receptive field in Figure 3.6 and noting that it seems to have something to do with detecting edges is not enough. We need to know why it has a Mexican Hat shape of excitation and inhibition, rather than say a Top Hat shape, or some other shape. That leads to asking precise questions about the nature of the edge point detection task that it is involved in solving.

Readers who want to know more about Marr and Hildreth's theory of Mexican Hat receptive fields might find it helpful to consult the review given by Mayhew and Frisby (1984) before tackling the original paper, particularly if they are not mathematically trained. Mayhew and Frisby also describe the role that Marr and Hildreth's theory gives to the simple cells discovered by Hubel and Wiesel (1962).

Before leaving this topic, it must be emphasized that the Marr/Hildreth theory is controversial, both as a theory of edge point detection and as a theory of Mexican Hat receptive fields. It is mentioned here not because it is 'correct'—only time will judge that—but because it nicely illustrates the kind of approach adopted by Marr in his attempts to interpret neurophysiological findings in computational terms. (For neurophysiological findings see also Part II, Section 3.1.)

2.3   Computing the full primal sketch

Reference has already been made to the local pointillist nature of the edge points of the raw primal sketch. But when we look at these points in Figure 3.5(b) we as humans readily see large-scale edges forming the boundaries of objects. It thus seems that a sensible next step for a visual system is to group the edge points of the raw primal sketch together so as to make explicit large-scale boundaries and lines. This step is still within the domain of the primal sketch because it is concerned with describing the intensity changes in a 2D image.

Before going on to describe how the large-scale boundaries of the full primal sketch might be extracted, it is as well to note that, for reasons of space, we have neglected to describe the early grouping processes that were envisaged by Marr in arriving at the raw primal sketch primitives other than edge points (namely small blobs, edge segments, and terminations). The latter primitives would also be available for the grouping processes of the full primal sketch.

Input representation   The output of the processes creating the raw primal sketch, that is edge point assertions making explicit the location and slopes of local intensity changes in the image, blobs, edge segments, and terminations. For simplicity, we will hereafter mention just edge points, but the reader should be aware of the full range of raw primal sketch primitives available.

Output representation   A rich multi-layed structure asserting the curvilinear organization of regions and boundaries within the image. Its primitives, like those of the raw primal sketch from which they are derived, are called *place tokens* because they 'stand for' things occurring at different places in the image (Marr, 1976). However, full primal sketch primitives are concerned with much larger image entities than the edge points and other primitives of the raw primal sketch.

The computational problem   The attempt to group together edge points belonging to the same image entities runs headlong into an ambiguity problem: often a given edge point could belong to two or more structures. For example, consider the alternative ways of grouping the dots shown in Figure 3.7. The grouping shown in Figure 3.7a

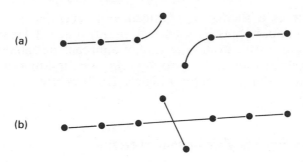

Figure 3.7   Two possible groupings of the same dots to demonstrate the grouping ambiguity problem

represents two separate curved edges, whereas the grouping in Figure 3.7b represents two intersecting straight edges. Similar sorts of choices would have to be made in trying to group edge points of the raw primal sketch into lines defining the boundaries of possible image entities.

The computational theory   The problem can be solved by a careful analysis of the nature of the world being viewed and the image structures that it is likely to present. Because the entities in the world are not typically a random collection of small dots (a snow storm would be an exception to this generalization), it would be sensible for our visual system to resolve ambiguities using a set of *grouping rules* based on this fact. For example, edges of objects are usually continuous, so it makes sense to choose edge point groupings which display maximum continuity, as well as proximity, i.e. being close together. Also, object edges or surface markings are usually similar in their characteristics, which justifies grouping together edge points of similar type.

In short, computing the full primal sketch provides a functional role for the well-known *Gestalt* grouping principles of *proximity*, *figural similarity*, *continuity*, *closure*, etc., including those mediating the perception of texture differences (Julesz, 1981; Pomerantz, 1985). Viewed from this perspective, the reason the Gestalt phenomena exist is that the mechanisms that implement them take advantage of the nature of the objects in our visual world to solve the computational problem of grouping together local dots that belong to the same 'thing'. The computed 'thing' is, in the literature of the psychology of vision, usually called the *figure* and its background is called the *ground*.

There is nothing very technical or sophisticated about the above theory. Indeed, some would perhaps feel the phrase 'computational theory' rather grand to apply to such an analysis. However, it is clear that the concerns being dealt with are to do with the nature of the visual task, and hence it fits our definition. Also, it should be borne in mind that the design of a computer program capable of carrying out such groupings often becomes highly technical (Mayhew and Frisby, 1984). Such details are beyond our scope but it is worth mentioning that, in implementing Gestalt grouping rules, it has proved valuable to employ two broad strategic computational principles that have had wide application in computer vision and AI generally (Marr, 1976).

The first of these is the *Principle of Explicit Naming*: if you want to manipulate a 'thing', or describe 'it', or reason about 'it', begin by giving 'it' a name. The names in question here would be 'regions', 'lines', etc. Figure 3.8 (overleaf) illustrates the principle at work in the case of grouping operations creating the full primal sketch. Various edge points are shown grouped together because they display proximity, figural continuity, and closure: the resulting 'things' are called 'regions' and the symbol R used as the label for place tokens which assert that a region has been found at such and such a location (expressed in terms of x,y image coordinates). Different regions are distinguished with a different number. Next, it is discovered that the R symbols (regions) can in turn be grouped together, because they satisfy the grouping principle of co-linearity. These then form a new set of place tokens, given the label L for 'lines'.

Here then is an example of a sequence of grouping operations, each stage based upon the Principle of Explicit Naming—once a name (symbol) has been given to an image entity, the symbol can be used in repeated applications of grouping operations to arrive at larger and larger entities. The Principle of Explicit Naming is, however, of much broader strategic significance than the present examples would suggest. It captures the essence of symbolic computation and hence underpins the whole enterprise of Artificial Intelligence. More will be said about symbols in Section 5.1.

The second guiding strategy is the *Principle of Least Commitment*: don't do anything that you might later have to undo—that is too costly and too difficult. In the present case, this principle is implemented by a sequence of applications of the grouping rules, beginning with a strict demand that the configurations of edge point dots fit very well, say, the grouping rule of figural continuity; otherwise the ambiguity is left unresolved (the system remains 'uncommitted' to any grouping). Then, as some of the competing possibilities are taken out by the strict application of the rule, so it becomes possible to employ less stringent demands safely for the remaining points. In short, it has been found that it is safest to apply the grouping rules in a manner which progressively reduces the similarity demanded as the computation proceeds.

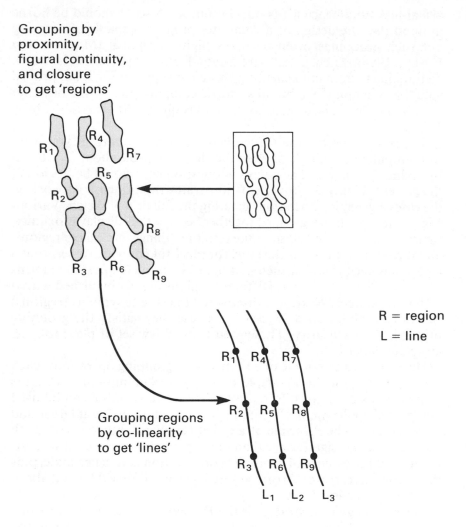

Figure 3.8   Grouping edge points to form primitives of the full primal sketch

Various types of algorithms can be used for grouping purposes but one important general class bears the name *relaxation algorithms*. These have been found useful whenever it is necessary to disambiguate, in a gradual and sensible manner, possible links between a mass of interacting local elements so as to achieve a labelling of those elements (e.g. a label of the type that says 'elements $a, k, p \ldots$ all belong to the same entity'). A detailed example of a relaxation algorithm at work will be given later in connection with the stereo correspondence problem.

Summary of Section 2

- A grey level description is obtained from the input light image by photochemical/electrical processes in the light-sensitive surface of a suitable optical device. The grey level description represents the light image as a 2D array of pixels. Each pixel is a number encoding the value of light at a point in the image. The size of the area of the image represented by each pixel determines the resolution of the grey level description.
- From the grey level description is computed the raw primal sketch. This shows the location and characteristics of edge point primitives representing intensity changes in the image.
- Marr and Hildreth's theory of the edge detecting problem is consistent with the antagonistic centre–surround properties of visual cells found in the early stages of a wide range of biological visual systems.
- The raw primal sketch is used as input for the computation of the full primal sketch. The latter represents the locations, boundary shapes, and texture properties of larger sized regions in the image derived from groupings of the edge points of the raw primal sketch.
- The processes which derive the full primal sketch have to choose between competing (ambiguous) potential groupings of edge points. They do this by applying Gestalt grouping principles to those edge segments.
- Two general principles are used in implementing grouping operations, namely the Principle of Explicit Naming, and the Principle of Least Commitment.

3   Stage 2: Computing surface descriptions—the 2.5D sketch

So far we have grappled with the problems of finding interesting (i.e. potentially useful) entities in the image. But the computer vision system we have set out to try and build has no idea yet what these 'things' are that it has grouped together and named with some provisional label. Moreover, it has not yet begun to tackle the problem of discovering the three-dimensional (3D) spatial layout of the surfaces in the viewed scene that have given rise to the 2D image structures it has found. It is to this latter task that we turn next.

Before doing so, it is worth pointing out that perhaps the most distinctive characteristic of the Image Understanding (IU) approach to computer vision is its commitment to computing a rich set of scene surface representations lying in between the early image/edge descriptions in the primal sketch and later representations serving the high level goal of object recognition. These intermediate level representations provide descriptions of the properties of visible surfaces in the scene, their distances, slants, boundaries, overlaps, reflectances, intensities of illumination falling on them, etc.

A term that has been coined by Marr for a multiply-cued representation of visible surfaces encoding the various properties listed above, is the *2.5D sketch*. That term was chosen because this kind of representation describes surfaces in a scene from the vantage point of the viewer, i.e. it is *viewpoint-dependent* (hence 'sketch'), and because it does not deliver a 'full 3D' description of the volumes in space occupied by the objects present in the scene. That is, the 2.5D sketch does not incorporate knowledge of object surfaces that are hidden from the particular view being analysed (the rather strange label '2.5D' tries to bring out this consideration). In contrast, a representation of the volumes occupied by known 3D objects would contain knowledge of surfaces that could be expected from views other than the one immediately in question.

The ability of the human visual system to deliver surface representations is magnificent, as a glance at the scene around you will quickly confirm. One of the major goals of IU is to understand this visual competence, which is one reason why IU has deep roots in the psychology of visual perception.

A great deal of research has examined the many cues that images provide about the depth layout of surfaces in a scene. From a long list of possibilities, which includes texture, shading, motion, shape and stereo vision, only the latter will be chosen for exposition. One reason for this is that Marr contributed greatly to the field of designing stereo algorithms.

3.1   Computing a range map surface representation from stereo projections

The human visual system is equipped with two optical devices, that is, two eyes, so that there are two retinal images available for processing. These images are not identical; they provide two slightly different projections of the same scene, called *stereo projections*. Figures 3.9a and 3.9b depict a pair of stereo projections (left and right images) arising from our familiar blocks scene. Careful inspection of these will reveal that they are slightly different. These differences are caused by the slightly different viewpoints of the two cameras that were used to record them (equivalent to differences in left and right

(a) Pair of stereo images (grey levels)

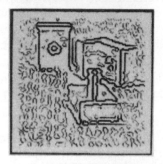

(b) Raw primal sketches (right and left images)

Feint = far

Dark = near

(c) Range map — first step to 2.5D sketch

Figure 3.9   Stereo vision: a stereo pair of left eye/right eye grey level descriptions (a) and raw primal sketches (b); information from disparities measured between the pair of raw primal sketches has been used to obtain the single binocular raw primal sketch shown in (c) in which each edge point has tagged to it a disparity value (coded as *far = light* and *near = dark*). N.B. The stereo pairs are arranged so that if you try crossed-eye fusion (so that the image on the left side of the page enters the right eye and the image on the right side of the page enters the left eye), then you should be able to see the scene in stereoscopic depth. Not all observers find this easy. (See Frisby, 1979, p. 145 for further advice on how to obtain this effect.)

eye positions in the head). The differences between images are known as *disparities* and they constitute a rich source of information about the depth structure of the scene. For example, the disparities can be used to generate what is known as a *range map*. This is a point-by-point description of a visual scene with a depth value tied to each point.

Figure 3.9 illustrates the basic idea. It shows how the raw primal sketches derived from the left and right grey level images can be combined to produce a single representation, which Mayhew and Frisby (1981) have called a *binocular raw primal sketch*. This is created by finding each matching edge point in the left and right raw primal sketches (Figure 3.9b) and computing a new parameter which is the disparity between their spatial positions in each sketch. Disparities of edge points that signal 'far away' are depicted in Figure 3.9c with light shading, disparities of edge points 'near at hand' are shown by dark shading, with a graded sequence of greys showing disparities in between. Now, if these disparity values were converted into actual distances, in say centimetres from the cameras, then we would have a range map of the scene. It is that kind of representation that we set out to compute in this section.

Input representation   Two raw primal sketches representing the location of edge points in two images taken from slightly different viewing positions. Other primal sketch primitives such as those representing dots or line segments might also be useful but in most of what follows attention will be restricted to edge point primitives.

Output representation   A range map making explicit the local depth structure of the scene using as primitives edge points, to which a depth value has been attached as a parameter.

The computational problem   There are several sub-problems which need to be solved in order to use disparities to generate a range map.
1 *Image registration*—the alignment of the two cameras/eyeballs needs to be appropriately adjusted so that they focus on the same fixation point and have the correct orientation with respect to one another and the scene being viewed.
2 *Correspondence*—the primitives derived from each image need to be matched and their disparities measured; the problem here is ambiguity in knowing which left image edge point matches which right image edge point.
3 *Interpretation*—the disparities need to be used to build up a range map of points lying on surfaces in the scene.
Although it is convenient to distinguish these sub-problems in a list, they are in fact quite closely coupled. Only the second will be dealt with here, and then only in a limited way.

The computational theory of the stereo correspondence problem   The classic illustration of the *stereo ambiguity problem* is shown in Figure 3.10b (based on Julesz, 1971). Figure 3.10a depicts a 'random-dot stereogram', i.e. a stereo pair comprising two visual fields of seemingly randomly positioned dots. Despite there being no recognizable form in either member of the stereo pair viewed alone, when the two halves are binocularly combined by the human visual system, using a stereoscope or by crossing the eyes, a vivid depth percept appears. In the case of the particular random-dot stereogram shown in Figure 3.10a, the depth percept is of a rippled surface with horizontal corrugations of different amplitudes.

The problem which such a random dot stereogram brings to the fore is: which dot in the left image goes with which in the right? How is one view to be mapped on to the other? Obviously, a large ambiguity

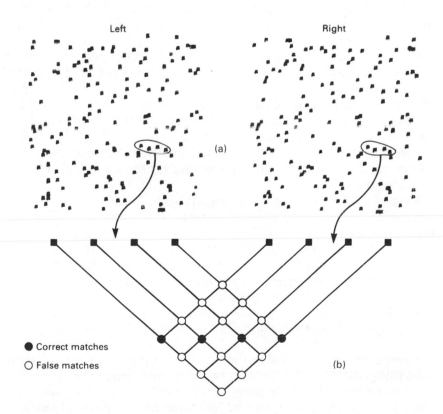

Figure 3.10   Correspondence problem: matching of dots between left and right halves of a random-dot stereogram (adapted from Julesz, 1971)

157

problem exists, as shown in Figure 3.10b, which depicts all possible matches between a sample of four dots taken from the right image with four dots taken from the left. Each possible match is shown as a node in a network formed by the intersections of lines drawn from each dot.

To understand this network, follow down the line from the left-hand dot from the left image. Each of the possible matches it can form with the four dots from the right image is shown as a circle. The question is: which of these possible matches is the correct one? The same question can be asked for all the other possible matches that can be formed for all the other dots. Now there are in fact 24 possible ways of combining sets of four dots such that each dot is allowed to participate in one and only one match ($4! = 4 \times 3 \times 2 = 24$). The stereo matching problem is to choose which combination is the correct one for the particular scene being viewed. That is not easy, especially when it is remembered that sets of four dots have been chosen here only for illustration — much larger sets would often need to be considered by a practical stereo matching system capable of dealing with richly textured surfaces.

For the particular stereogram shown in Figure 3.10a, the correct matches for the chosen sample set of four dots are depicted by nodes in the network shown as filled-in circles. They happen to be the correct matches in this case simply because they are the ones that reflect the surface depicted in the stereogram for the region in question. If the stereogram had been set up to portray some other surface then a different combination of matches would have been 'correct'. Note that all the 'false' matches for the present case are shown in Figure 3.10b by unfilled circles.

Despite the ambiguity in matching left/right image elements, which occurs for stereo image pairs of natural scenes like that shown in Figure 3.9a as well as for artificial random-dot stereograms, the human visual system nevertheless usually succeeds in combining the two images correctly. To design a *stereo correspondence algorithm* capable of achieving comparable performance requires the specification of rules for guiding binocular combination that are well-founded on an appropriate analysis of the stereo correspondence task. Marr and Poggio (1976) based their analysis on the following considerations.

1 Compatibility   The goal of the stereo combination process is to say something useful about entities in the scene; hence the primitives extracted from each of the images to be used for matching purposes must correspond to well-defined locations on the physical surfaces being imaged. From this follows Binocular Combination Rule 1: elements are allowed to form a potential match if they could have arisen from the same surface marking. What this amounts to is that nodes in the ambiguity diagram (Figure 3.10b) can only be established for pairings of left and right image primitives with figurally similar parameters. For the particular stereo pair shown in Figure 3.10a, suitable matching primitives would be ones describing small black dots, and as the black dots are in this example everywhere alike, any primitive could in this case in principle be matched with any other. But suppose the surface depicted by the stereo pair had been grey in colour and speckled with some black and some white dots. Then Binocular Combination Rule 1 would preclude considering matches formed from black/white dot pairings, as these could not arise from the same surface marking in normal stereo projections.

Obviously, the edge points of the raw primal sketch would be one kind of matching primitive that would allow the requirements of Rule 1 to be met for many natural scenes (Figure 3.9). For example, right and left image edge points could be allowed to form matches if they had roughly the same orientation, same scale (steep or shallow intensity change), and same direction of intensity change (an edge point describing a bright-to-dark intensity change in a given region of one image could be matched with a bright-to-dark one from the other image but not with a dark-to-bright one).

Note that Marr and Poggio did not make Rule 1 fully explicit in their 1976 paper but Marr does so in his book (Marr, 1982, p. 114) where his treatment of the issue is close to that of Mayhew and Frisby (1981).

2 Uniqueness   A given point on a physical surface has a unique position in space at any one time. This leads to Binocular Combination Rule 2: matches should be selected in such a way that any given matching primitive derived from one image should be allowed to participate in one and only one of the selected matches. To break this rule would be tantamount to allowing a surface marking to be in two places at the same time.

3 Surface smoothness   Due to the fact that matter is cohesive (it occurs in fairly large chunks — our normal visual world is not a swarm of gnats or a snow storm), the surfaces of objects are generally smooth (compared with their distance from the viewer). In other words, neighbouring points on a surface are likely to be similar in their depths away from the viewer. This provides Binocular Combination Rule 3: give preference to matches that have neighbouring matches with similar disparities. That is, choose matches such that, as far as possible, disparities vary smoothly across them.

A stereo algorithm

Reference was made in Section 1 to the claim that complex information processing systems need to be understood not only at the computational theory and hardware levels but also at the algorithm level (recollect that an algorithm is a set of procedures which specify in detail a sequence of operations that achieve a given end). Hence attention will be turned next to devising a detailed set of procedures for stereo matching based upon the three binocular combination rules specified by the computational theory. The algorithm chosen for illustrative purposes is an abbreviated and simplified form of the one described by Marr and Poggio (1976; see also Marr, 1982, for a fairly complete yet not very technical account of this algorithm).

1 Set up a *network* of *nodes* representing all possible disparity matches covering the depth range required. Give a value of 1 to each node representing a possible match between figurally similar place tokens derived from the two stereo images. Set all other nodes to a value of zero. Nodes with a value of 1 are hereafter called 'active'.

2 For each node in the network, count up how many of its neighbouring nodes at the same disparity are active. In Figure 3.10b, these are the active neighbours lying in the same horizontal row as the node being considered. However, the algorithm needs to count active same-disparity neighbours in all directions around the node in question (Figure 3.11). Call this count the 'Same-disparity Count'.

3 For each node in the network, count up how many active nodes there are on each line passing through the node being considered. Call this count the 'Alternatives Count' (because matches on these lines, sometimes called the 'lines of sight' for each primitive, define the set of all possible alternative matches for the image primitives in question).

4 Subtract the Alternatives Count from the Same-disparity Count to gain a measure of the 'strength of support' for the match represented by each node. In Figure 3.11, the support is +2 for the node shown.

5 Define a suitable threshold value for the strength of support that a node must have if it is to remain active, or if it is to become active (some nodes might have had no matching primitives to set them active at the outset, e.g. if the texture is sparse, but nevertheless gain sufficient support from same-disparity neighbours to exceed the threshold; this leads to the algorithm filling-in blank areas of ground—compare similar effects in human stereo vision, Julesz and Frisby, 1975). Set all nodes that exceed the threshold to a value of 1. Set all nodes with below threshold strength to zero.

6 Repeat Steps 2 to 5 until the network has converged to a stable state in which few if any nodes change from active to inactive, or vice

versa, in each repetition (known technically as each 'iteration').
7 Nodes active at the stable endpoint are deemed to be those
  representing 'correct' binocular matches.

A name often used for this sort of algorithm is *cooperative* because
the solution is determined by interactions between many cooperating
elements (here nodes). The term 'cooperative algorithm' is often used
interchangeably with 'relaxation algorithm'. (Algorithms of this general
class have been used to implement the kind of grouping rules described

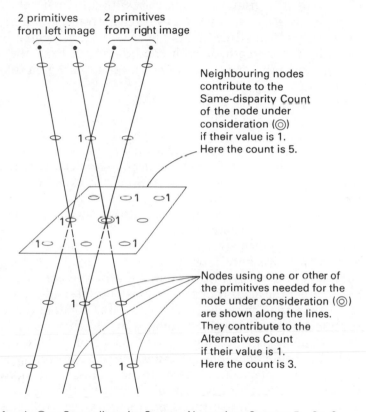

Strength of node ⊚ = Same-disparity Count − Alternatives Count = 5 − 3 = 2

Figure 3.11   Marr and Poggio's stereo algorithm: a sample of the nodes
comprising the disparity network. Nodes on the lines define the possible
matches for each primitive (not all lines are shown for reasons of clarity).
If their value is 1 then it means that two primitives exist which can form
a possible match at that node. Support from neighbouring nodes at the same
disparity (shown as being in the same horizontal plane) outweighs
contradictory evidence from nodes (shown on lines) with different disparities
sharing one or other primitive

in Section 2, by setting up a network such that nodes representing the grouping with strongest neighbourhood support in terms of figural continuity, etc., are the ones which win out in the end.)

The above algorithm attempts to implement the three binocular combination rules provided by the Marr/Poggio computational theory as follows:

Rule 1 (Compatibility) is embedded in Step 1 in that initially active nodes are restricted to those representing figurally similar matches. Rule 3 (Smoothness) is implemented by the Same-disparity Count (Step 4) as this ensures that matches with a large number of similar-disparity neighbours will tend to be the strongest and hence survive the threshold cut. Rule 2 (Uniqueness) is implemented in Step 6 by reducing the strength of each candidate match by the Alternative Count: doing that tends to suppress all but one match for each image primitive.

Having set out the steps to be followed in the algorithm, the next task is to write a computer program which executes them and see if the algorithm actually does solve the stereo correspondence problem. That would lead to some experimentation in choosing a suitable threshold value (Step 5) and a suitable size for the area over which the Same-disparity Count is taken (Step 2; it would be foolish to have too large an area as the Smoothness constraint upon which this count depends refers to neighbouring points on surfaces as having similar depths, not very distant ones).

In exploring the performance of the algorithm, many issues would arise which are only loosely related, if at all, to the underlying computational theory. For example, in the present case one needs to ask whether the algorithm converges to a stable end-point without too many time-consuming iterations. Also, one might ask whether simply subtracting the Alternatives Count is an effective way of insisting on each primitive participating finally in only one of the selected matches (Rule 3). These questions are examples of algorithm level problems. Finding solutions to them needs to be guided by the computational theory but they are to be kept distinct from the theory itself. After all, if this particular algorithm did not work very well, this would not necessarily imply that the binocular combination rules were themselves inadequate—it could simply be that the algorithm does not take proper advantage of them. In fact, partly because he grew to dislike iterative algorithms for various reasons (Marr, 1982, p. 107), Marr and Poggio devised a second non-iterative stereo algorithm of a radically different nature from the present one even though it was based on the same three constraints as the first (Marr and Poggio, 1979). This fact brings out the value of distinguishing between computational theory and algorithm.

Tests of algorithms like the one just described have shown that they can solve the stereo correspondence problem quite successfully for simple scenes composed of flat surfaces whose orientation is parallel to the line joining the eyes/cameras (surfaces said to lie in 'fronto-parallel' planes). But what of other surfaces, for example surfaces slanting away in depth from the viewer? Using a Same-disparity Count of active neighbours is unsuitable for them because the neighbours of correct matches in those cases will have few if any same-disparity neighbours—even if the surfaces are smooth and hence in keeping with the Smoothness constraint. This criticism points up the limited nature of Marr and Poggio's implementation in the present type of algorithm of the constraints identified in their own computational theory.

But one can criticize more deeply and ask whether the smoothness constraint is itself really satisfactory: is it really true to say that the world is generally smooth, even if slants are allowed? Many commonplace objects, such as bushes, hair, or tufted carpets, present very jagged surfaces in depth and yet they can be fused very nicely by human stereo vision. Are these just to be regarded as degenerate cases or is there something fundamentally wrong with the theory?

The pursuit of the question is currently a research issue. Pollard, Mayhew and Frisby (1985) provide an alternative stereo theory that can cope with both smooth and jagged surfaces, and they describe a stereo algorithm based upon it. Their theory was stimulated by some psychophysical findings on human vision and their algorithm may well bear some resemblance to one of those used by human vision. Limitations of space preclude describing that work but its good performance on stereo images of the industrial blocks scene is illustrated in Figure 3.9c.

Biological hardware for Marr and Poggio's stereo algorithm

Supposing for the purposes of exposition that the Marr/Poggio stereo theory and the algorithm just described were satisfactory, at least for a limited range of surface types if not in general: how then might the algorithm be implemented in biological hardware? One of the attractive features of the algorithm is that it lends itself readily to implementation in a network of nerve cells. It is worth describing how it does so briefly by way of illustrating Marr's distinction between the different levels needed for analysing complex information processing systems—computational theory, algorithm, and hardware.

Imagine replacing each of the abstract nodes of Figure 3.10b with a neurone, so that now a brain cell is used directly to represent each of the possible matches, with its activity (e.g. firing rate in nerve

163

impulses per second) coding the strength of support for the match in question. Moreover, imagine the lines in the diagram to be replaced with nerve fibres capable of carrying messages between cells about the current activity of each cell. If the connections these fibres made with each cell were arranged to be inhibitory, then this hardware implements Step 5 of the algorithm — subtracting the Alternatives Count. The idea here is that if one cell is 'on' then it has the right to tell all others using one or other of 'its' primitives to 'be quiet, you can't be right if I am right!'. Implementing the Same-disparity Count (Step 4) can be easily achieved by putting in some more fibres, this time ones that link neighbouring same-disparity cells with excitatory connections. Here the idea is that cells which are on should say to their same-disparity neighbours: 'I am on, so the chances are that you should be on also, so here is some excitation to help you survive!'. The iterative repetitions could be implemented by simply allowing the network of cells to battle it out, as it were, to see which cells survive at the end of the day — in practice, of course, hopefully after only a few tens of milliseconds.

The speculative neurones described above may or may not bear any deep similarity to the disparity-sensitive neurones that have been discovered in the brains of many animals using single unit recording techniques (e.g. Barlow, Blakemore and Pettigrew, 1967). Just what those real neurones are computing is still not known, but the chances of finding out are increasing as neurophysiologists interested in disparity processing are now starting to cast their work within a framework which asks: what is the computational problem that this or that neurone might be solving? Poggio and Poggio (1984) provide a good review of the neurophysiology of the field considered in that way.

Meanwhile, it has to be said that regrettably little, if anything, has emerged so far from the neurophysiological literature that has contributed much to the design of a good stereo algorithm — a sobering thought for those who believe that 'the truth lies in the hardware'. On the other hand, a great deal of guidance has come from the psychophysics of binocular vision (Poggio and Poggio, 1984, and Mayhew and Frisby, 1981, provide reviews.)

3.2   Computing surface descriptions from the range map

A range map gives only local point-by-point depth information about surfaces in the scene. It is therefore at a rather primitive level of analysis as far as the goals of computing a 2.5D sketch are concerned. The next step is to group together related parts of the range map into useful higher-level descriptive entities, such as a concave (or convex) junction between two surfaces (an edge), or a concave (or convex) junction between three or more surfaces (a *vertex*, e.g. a corner). These types of 2.5D sketch primitives are illustrated in Figure 3.12 for a line drawing of a block. Figure 3.13 (overleaf) illustrates the task to be faced in deriving them from the range map that was the output of the stereo algorithm in Figure 3.9c.

Note that, as for primal sketch primitives, each one would need to carry a suitable set of parameters defining its particular shape characteristics and its location. It is difficult to be more specific about such primitives at the present time because their recovery is right at the forefront of research.

In addition to edges and vertices, some description of the shape of the surface patches that form them is clearly desirable. For example, subsequent stages concerned with object recognition will need to know whether such surfaces are cylindrical, spherical, planar, or whatever. One approach that has been considered for the first stages of recovering such descriptions is to compute the orientation in depth of each location on a surface. One way of doing this is illustrated in Figure 3.12 where

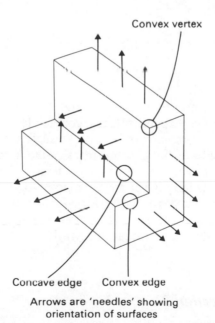

Convex vertex

Concave edge   Convex edge

Arrows are 'needles' showing
orientation of surfaces

Figure 3.12   2.5D sketch: identification of surface features—junctions of two surfaces to form edges and three or more surfaces to form vertices (corners as illustrated). The orientation of local surface patches is shown by a needle map of surface normals (perpendiculars)

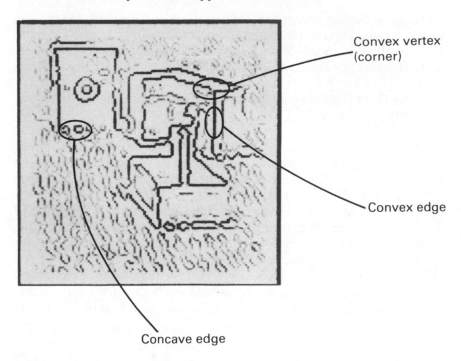

Convex vertex
(corner)

Convex edge

Concave edge

Figure 3.13 2.5D sketch: identification of edge junctions and vertices from edge points in raw primal sketch

arrows are shown pointing at right angles from the surfaces of the block to indicate the perpendiculars (technically the *surface normals*). If perpendiculars were shown for all the surfaces in the scene (as in Figure 3.12), one has what is sometimes called a *needle map* showing the orientation of every part of every surface. This is fine as far as it goes but a needle map is yet another point-by-point representation and its elements need to be grouped together into larger scale descriptions of the properties of surfaces. Once again, we have come to a current highly active research frontier.

Summary of Section 3

● Using the primal sketch as input, the next representation to be computed is referred to as the 2.5D sketch.
● A 2.5D sketch describes the surfaces in the scene from the vantage point of the viewer: it does not represent object surfaces that are hidden in the particular view being analysed.

- One way of deriving the depth structure of visible surfaces is to use stereo vision. Disparities between the left and right images can be used to build up a range map of the scene, that is, a point-by-point description of the scene with a depth value tagged to each point.
- The stereo correspondence problem is how to resolve ambiguities in matching up primitives extracted from the left and right images. Marr and Poggio (1976) solved this problem for certain types of surface using a stereo algorithm which took advantage of three constraints: compatibility, uniqueness and surface smoothness.
- A description of visible surfaces can be computed from a range map by grouping together related parts of the map into higher level 2.5D sketch primitives which describe junctions between surfaces (edge and vertex features). Other higher level primitives represent the shape-in-depth of the surfaces bounded by surface junctions. A first step towards obtaining the latter primitives might be to compute a needle map describing the orientation in depth of surfaces in terms of surface normals.

4   Stage 3: Computing object descriptions

The surface descriptions that comprise the 2.5D sketch would be immediately useful for a number of visual tasks. For example, they make explicit information about the depth structure of the scene which would be useful input for, say, a computer program designed to guide a driver-less vehicle. They would also do for planning collision-free trajectories for a robot arm being moved through a pile of objects on a table. And if the surface descriptions were sufficiently rich and the viewpoint good enough, they might be suitable for planning a possible place to grasp a target object without the robot needing to know what the 'thing' is that it is about to pick up. But in general, and certainly for the task of automatic assembly of industrial parts, it is desirable to build into a visual system the capability for recognizing the objects with which it has to deal. In this context, recognition means matching an input shape to one of a stored collection of object models. Once recognition has been attained, information stored about the object, such as the nature of its surfaces that are not visible from the current viewpoint, can be used to guide further visual processing and for planning suitable actions.

The objects with which we are trying to deal occupy a volume of space whose shape is characterized by the disposition in space of its visible surfaces. Hence, it is natural to consider ways of using the surface descriptions in the 2.5D sketch as a database for object recognition. It is worth bearing in mind, however, that a good many practical 3D object recognition schemes, including the 'toy blocks world' approach discussed in Part II, use as their input the kind of information delivered by the 2D primal sketch, not least because the problems of obtaining a decent 2.5D sketch have yet to be solved.

Input representation   Primitives in the 2.5D sketch representing the shape and depth properties of visible surfaces.

Output representation   Primitives representing the shape of a 3D object. This shape representation must be capable of being matched to one of a stored collection of 3D object models.

The computational problem   Marr and Nishihara (1978) listed three criteria that must be met by a 'good' representation of a 3D shape:
1 *Accessibility:* Can the representation be computed easily?
2 *Scope and Uniqueness:* Is the type of representation suitable for the class of shapes with which it has to deal (*Scope*); and do the shapes in that class have one or more canonical representations (*Uniqueness*)? A *canonical representation* is one in which a particular shape has a single description in the representation, that is, all the different views of the same object produce the same shape description. For example, the shape of a 'tin of beans' may be described as 'two flat round surface patches joined to the edges of a cyclindrical surface'; this description would apply regardless of the viewing angle (as long as the tin had not been opened, of course!). A representation with this property is obviously advantageous for matching purposes.
    A non-canonical representation on the other hand, would be one which produced different representations depending on the viewpoint. For example, a scheme of this type for a tin of beans might contain a list of representations for different viewpoints, such as 'flat circular patch' when the view is along the central axis, and 'convex cylindrical patch' when the tin is viewed side on. This type of scheme leads to the need for additional processes capable of solving the critical problem of matching all the possible views to the single object model for a tin of beans stored in memory.
3 *Stability and Sensitivity:* Can the representation be used to capture both the similarities (*Stability*) and the differences (*Sensitivity*) between the objects with which it has to deal? For example, we can

readily see that a horse and a donkey share some properties in common as well having some (potentially important) differences. A good object representation scheme must lend itself naturally to delivering these opposing but complementary requirements. This demands a separation of the invariant information characterizing a particular category of shapes from information about the subtle differences between shapes in the same category.

Marr and Nishihara then went on to show how these general criteria are useful for guiding the search for solutions to three design problems that have to be faced in building a 3D shape representation, namely:

1 What are the *primitives* that will be used to describe shapes?

2 In what *coordinate system* are the spatial relationships between primitives to be located?

3 What is an appropriate *organization* of the primitives?

We will consider each of these in turn.

4.1   Primitives

What elementary units should be used to describe any given object? Should the 'visual primitives' for describing objects refer to surface properties or should they describe explicitly the volume properties of the space occupied by the object?

Consider once more the shape of a tin of beans. In the examples given earlier, surface-based primitives were used to describe it as 'two flat round surface patches joined to the edges of a cylindrical surface'. To this would need to be added information about the absolute and relative sizes of the surface primitives (so that the tin of beans would not be confused with a flagpole, for example). This example amounts to describing an object in terms of relationships between 2.5D sketch primitives.

An alternative scheme based on *volumetric primitives* called *generalized cylinders* is illustrated in Figure 3.14. Here the underlying idea is to find an axis within the volume occupied by each part of the object, and then define the surface of the object in terms of a cross-section of a particular shape moved along that axis. This cross-section may vary smoothly in size and shape along the axis, and the axis need not remain straight along its length (think of a banana)—hence the term 'generalized cylinders'. It would also be necessary to specify the relative lengths of the axes, in order, for instance, to distinguish once again between the shapes of a tin of beans and a flagpole. A key point to grasp here is that an axis-based representation makes explicitly available for immediate use certain volumetric properties of a shape

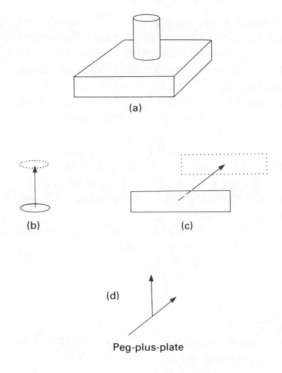

Figure 3.14   Volumetric primitives: the peg in (a) is represented in (b) as an axis with a round cross-section, swept along it; the plate in (a) is represented in (c) as an axis with a rectangular cross-section swept along it. The two axes together in (d) represent the peg-plus-plate configuration in (a)

that would only be implicit in a surface-based description of, say, Figure 3.14a as a 'flat round patch joined to the edges of a cylindrical patch which is joined to a planar patch which is joined . . . etc.'.

It is easy to envisage how a complex object could in principle be described in terms of a collection of generalized cylinders connected together at certain points. The *peg-plus-plate* axis representation in Figure 3.14d shows the relationship between the axes of its two parts— how the axes for the two objects in 3.14b and 3.14c could be combined to represent the object in 3.14a. More complicated cases can readily be imagined by thinking of stick-figure drawings or pipe-cleaner sculptures of familiar animals. Indeed, the fact that the human visual system is so adept at recognizing an object depicted with such an immensely impoverished stimulus as a stick figure was one of the factors that led Marr and Nishihara to take very seriously the idea that our brains do actually compute axis-based volumetric 3D shape representations. Their argument runs: the reason we can 'see' a stick figure as depicting an object is that the human visual system generates stick-figure-like representations. So, when a stick figure is presented as a stimulus, it provides a short-cut, as it were, to the 3D representation normally computed from earlier representations such as the primal sketch and 2.5D sketch.

The criteria that have to be borne in mind in taking the decision to go for surface-based or volumetric primitives are 'Scope' and 'Uniqueness'. Not all objects lend themselves readily to generalized cylinders. A crumpled newspaper was Marr and Nishihara's illustration of a clearly unsuitable object (it could be described with so many alternative axes), but it could be that many important and commonplace objects are not well represented as generalized cylinders (would a typewriter be very easy to describe with them, or a telephone?).

On the other hand, it might prove easier to build canonical representations (meeting the Uniqueness criterion) using volumetric primitives. In principle (but the practical difficulties are considerable!), axis-based primitives allow an object to be represented by a single description of the spatial relations of the object's parts, a description arrived at from whatever angle the object is viewed. It is not clear that surface-based representations lend themselves so readily to canonical representations but one attempt to do so will be discussed in the next section.

4.2   Coordinate system

Whatever primitives are chosen, their spatial relationships one to another will be what determines the structure of any given shape description in the representation. To express those spatial relationships requires choosing a *coordinate system*. That is, a set of axes (x, y, z) need to be chosen for defining a 3D space in which the parts of an object can be localized. The immediate question that arises is should the coordinate system be *viewer-centred* (e.g. the origin of the coordinate frame located, say, at a point mid-way between the eyes of the viewer), or should it be *object-centred* (i.e. its origin located on some part of the object)?

A viewer-centred coordinate system is one which, as its name implies, expresses the spatial disposition of primitives from the viewpoint of the observer. This is easier to compute (i.e. satisfies the Accessibility criterion) but when used for recognition it will obviously be non-canonical (i.e. will fail the Uniqueness criterion), because it computes representations of many different viewpoint-determined descriptions.

Just how many might be required is not clear. Indeed, it is a current research question whether a scheme of this general sort can be made viable by restricting the infinitely large number of possible views to just a few typical or 'characteristic views' of each object that the visual system in question needs to be able to recognize. For example, you rarely need to recognize a car from underneath. This kind of thinking has a long history in the psychological literature on object recognition.

One important idea here is that of the 'view potential' of objects, introduced by Koenderink and van Doorn (1977). They observed that the qualitative character of many views of an object is often the same, that is they share the same main features even if these features might show some differences in quantitative details (e.g. due to perspective effects). Imagine walking around a detached house, for example, starting at the front. You would initially see the 'front view', which would include such features as the front door, front windows, eaves, perhaps a gable end. As you walked around from that starting point, nothing qualitative would change until a side elevation suddenly came into sight, whereupon a new 'front/side' view would arise comprising all the previous front-view features plus, say, a set of side windows, a side door, etc. Further walking round the house would bring you to a point where the front-view features were lost, leaving the side-view features on their own—the 'side view'. Given such qualitative jumps, the infinity of possible views seen from the ground plane can thus be grouped into only eight classes: front, front/side, side, side/back, back, back/side, side, side/front, as shown in Figure 3.15. Each one is canonical in the sense that a single description of it is computed from the infinity of possible viewpoints which can give rise to it. This realization presents an opportunity for creating a viewer-centred recognition scheme but one which reduces the number of views needing to be stored by using a limited number of canonical representations of characteristic views.

Koenderink and van Doorn employ the apt term *view potential* to bring out the fact that an object only has a limited number of qualitatively different views. While it may seem more difficult to specify a limited number of such views for less 'regular' objects than houses, the feasibility of this idea is now being explored in various AI labs. For further information about this sort of shape representation scheme, consult Koenderink and van Doorn (1977).

Of considerable biological interest in this connection are the recent findings of Perrett *et al.* (1985). They report evidence that viewer-centred descriptions may be computed in the temporal cortex of the macaque monkey, where they have found single neurones selectively responsive to different views of other monkeys' heads—full-face,

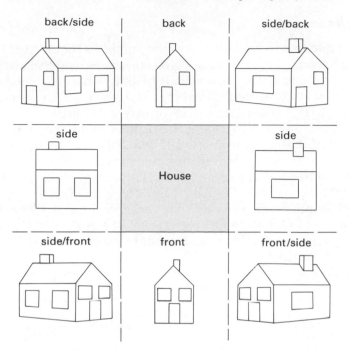

Figure 3.15   The view potential of a house showing the eight qualitatively different views available from viewing positions on the ground plane (after Koenderink and van Doorn)

profile, back or top of the head, face rotated 45 degrees up to the ceiling or down to the floor.

In contrast to the descriptions of surfaces from different view-points, an *object-centred coordinate system* expresses the relationships between primitives in a framework based upon some property of the object itself. For example, the simple peg-plus-plate axis description illustrated in Figure 3.14d uses the axis of the plate (representing the rectangular block) to define the location of the peg axis (representing the round block). It is because the plate axis is fixed by the nature of the object itself, and is therefore independent of viewpoint, that a scheme of this type is described as based on an object-centred coordinate system. The advantage of this kind of scheme is that it is canonical and hence facilitates recognition regardless of the viewer's particular viewpoints. On the other hand, this factor may be offset by the computational difficulties of computing object-centred descriptions from primal sketch and/or 2.5D sketch primitives (i.e. poor Accessibility).

4.3   Organization

The next question to consider is how the primitives should be organized in order to facilitate the recognition of objects. Should there be a 'flat' organizational structure, in which all primitives have an equal status? Or should there be a *hierarchical organization* in which primitives at the highest level convey coarse information about the shape of an object, with lower levels giving the details? A hierarchical scheme satisfies the Stability/Sensitivity criterion. This is because similarities at the highest level can deliver the competence to 'see' the sameness between a horse and donkey, or even a horse and tortoise, with lower levels in the hierarchy dealing with their differences. This organizational scheme has some similarities with the conceptual hierarchies proposed by Collins and Quillian and Rosch, described in Part I. An example of a hierarchical organization of volumetric primitives will be given in the next section.

4.4   A computational theory of 3D shape recognition

As the linking theme of Part III has been the work of Marr, it is natural to choose as an example of a computational theory of 3D shape recognition the one that he and Nishihara proposed. It should be emphasized, however, that many other candidates could have been selected for presentation and evaluated against the criteria they set out. Moreover, it is important to realize that the unsolved research problems in this field far exceed the successes.

Following on from their account of design choices and criteria, the 3D shape representation scheme proposed by Marr and Nishihara (1978) was object-centred, volumetric, hierarchical, and used generalized cylinders as its primitives. An outline of their scheme for describing the human form is illustrated in Figure 3.16 and described by them as follows:

> First the overall form — the 'body' — is given an axis. This yields an object-centred coordinate system which can then be used to specify the arrangement of the 'arms', 'legs', 'torso', and 'head'. The position of each of these is specified by an axis of its own, which in turn serves to define a coordinate system for specifying the arrangement of further subsidiary parts. This gives us a hierarchy of 3D models: we show it extending downward as far as the fingers. The shapes in the figure are drawn as if they were cylindrical, but that is purely for illustrative convenience: it is the axes alone that stand for the volumetric qualities of the shape, much as pipecleaner models can serve to describe various animals.   (Marr and Nishihara, 1978).

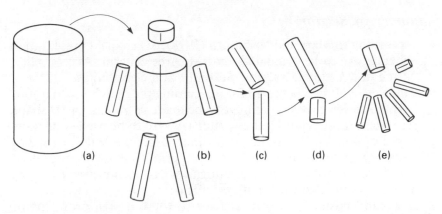

Figure 3.16 Hierarchical organization of generalized cylinders representing a human figure: (a) coarsest level — overall model axis; (b) axes representing parts at next level of resolution; the arm axis shown in (b) forms an overall model axis for its two component parts (upper and lower arm) shown in (c); the sequence continues with a lower arm model whose parts are fore-arm and hand (d), and a hand model whose parts are palm and fingers (e) (after Marr and Nishihara, 1978)

Marr and Nishihara never reached the point of fully implementing this scheme (see the ACRONYM program of Brooks, 1981, for the most advanced version of a generalized cylinder object representation to date). Moreover, they discussed the problems of computing generalized cylinders from the primal sketch rather than the 2.5D sketch. Although they believed that the 2.5D sketch would provide a better basis in principle, knowledge about how to compute surface descriptions of the required type and richness was not then available, and indeed is only slowly becoming available even now.

Note that the representation shown in Figure 3.16 is a kind of 'structural description' (see Part II), that is, a list of parts (cylinders) and the spatial relationships existing between them. The latter relationships were called by Marr and Nishihara the *adjunct relations*. Thus a person and a tailess horse might be regarded as having the same number of parts (a trunk, four limbs, a neck and a head) but they would be distinguished by differences in the admissible range of angles at which the component axes connected to the principle axis, as well as being distinguished in terms of the allowable relative sizes of the components. For further details of how they proposed the store of model objects could be accessed, see the original paper, or for an introduction, consult Mayhew and Frisby (1984).

Summary of Section 4

- According to Marr and Nishihara (1978), 3D shape representation schemes are to be evaluated against three criteria: Accessibility, Scope and Uniqueness, and Stability and Sensitivity.
- These general criteria are useful for guiding the search for solutions to three design choices that have to be made in building a 3D shape representation: What kind of primitives are to be used—surface-based or volumetric? What co-ordinate system should be used to represent spatial relationships between primitives—viewer-centred or object-centred? What organization of primitives is to be adopted—equal status or hierarchical?
- Marr and Nishihara's own answer to these design problems of object recognition was to extract a canonical volumetric 3D shape representation in terms of a hierarchically organized description of principle and component axes of generalized cylinders, their adjunct relations, and their relative sizes, to be matched to a model of the object stored in memory.
- Marr's representational framework for a general vision system is summarized in Table 3.1.

5   General issues in Image Understanding

5.1   Representations in Artificial Intelligence

It will already be clear that the notion of a representation is fundamental to the approach to vision adopted here. It will be as well therefore to pick out some of the most salient features of this concept as it is used in Artificial Intelligence (AI). Most of what will be said follows Winston (1984) who regards representation as the most serious issue to be faced in AI.

A visual representation, like a language representation, is a set of syntactic and semantic conventions that makes it possible to describe things in a given domain. The *syntax* specifies the symbols (primitives) that can be used, together with rules stating their allowable arrangements. The *semantics* specifies the meaning to be attributed to the symbol arrangements by showing the use to which they are put, that is, how the symbols can be used for getting something done.

A representation is thus a set of conventions about how to describe a class (domain) of things. A given description will make use of the conventions of the representation to describe some particular thing.

Table 3.1   Representational framework for a general purpose vision system (after Marr, 1982)

Name	Purpose		Input primitives	Output primitives
Grey level description	Represents intensity at each point in image		None (Input is light image)	Pixel numbers
Primal sketch	Makes explicit intensity changes of the image, and their geometrical distribution	R A W	Pixels	Edge points Blobs Terminations Edge segments
		F U L L	Edge points etc. of raw primal sketch	Groupings Curvilinear organization
2.5D sketch	Makes explicit the depth, orientation and junctions of visible surfaces in a viewer-centred coordinate frame		Edge points Blobs Terminations Edge segments	Range map Needle map of surface normals Shape of surface patches (cylindrical, planar, etc.) Edge junctions Vertex junctions
3D object module	Describes shapes and their spatial organization		Surface patch descriptions Edge junctions Vertex junctions	3D Models, for example (a) an object-centred volumetric and hierarchically organized set of 3D models, each one a spatial configuration of axes of generalized cylinders (b) surface-based representations of characteristic views (view potential)

The point of having a representation is that it allows some useful task to be accomplished, and the meaning of the representation is determined by what exactly that task is.

As an example of the above concepts, consider the edge point primitives of the raw primal sketch. These 'stand for' (hence the term 'place token') certain intensity variations in the image. If the assumption is made that the edge point tokens can be used for stereo matching in order to identify surfaces, then the semantic meaning of these tokens is defined as 'surface marking encoders'.

The reader should however be aware of the controversies that lurk behind the simplified overview of the concept of a representation just given. The biggest of these is whether a computer system that is able to perform some useful task using its symbolic representation can be said to have 'mind'. There are two main schools of thought on this question: one argues that 'clever' computer systems actually replicate mind (the strong AI hypothesis): the other that computer systems only simulate mind (the weak AI hypothesis). This issue is currently a hot topic amongst philosophers, workers in AI, psychologists, neurophysiologists, and others interested in considering the mind/brain problem in the light of the 'computer revolution' (Sloman, 1980).

This debate was publicized by Searle in the 1984 Reith Lectures where he argued that mind is not a property of all symbol-handling devices but emerges from (he says is 'caused by' or is 'a feature of') only some sorts of material, of which brain tissue is an example. He claims that no other sorts are yet known, but he is open to the idea that they might yet be discovered. He argues for that view while rejecting dualism — the notion that mind and matter are different sorts of substance.

For reasons which are obscure to me, Searle regards computers as logically outside the realm of mind-causing things, condemned forever to be limited by his definition of computers as syntax-operating devices. For Searle, computers quite simply do not have semantics and that is that. Unfortunately, he fails to consider seriously the AI conception of semantics outlined briefly above, which makes it problematic to know what his objection really amounts to. For a sophisticated discussion of semantics, see Johnson-Laird *et al.* (1984)

5.2   *Why bother with biological vision?*

The field of Image Understanding welcomes the study of biological vision systems, not only for their intrinsic interest, but also for the clues they might offer about good theories of visual tasks. The strategy of studying the best visual systems presently known hardly needs justification but, runs the IU argument, it must be done within a conceptual framework which recognizes the distinction between a theory of a task and details about how that theory might be implemented in a particular machine, natural or man-made. Merely studying intriguing biological 'phenomena' and positing explanatory 'mechanisms' (couched either in terms of the properties of neural units or in terms of the black box flow charts of many cognitive psychologists) is simply not good enough, unless these mechanisms are related to some analysis of a task carried out by the visual system. Only then can a perceptual phenomenon, say, a visual illusion, and the neural mechanisms producing it, be understood in the deepest and fullest sense. For instance, the illusion 'error' may only really be understood when it is interpreted as an inevitable 'cost' of using a constraint specified by a computational theory in circumstances which are not appropriate (Gregory, 1980; Marr, 1982).

These issues raise questions about the utility of the *software-hardware* distinction that some people have used as a metaphor for mind and brain. If this metaphor is intended to amount to the same thing as saying 'we need to know the computational theories implemented in the brain', then all well and good from the perspective on vision offered here. But it is far from clear that users of the software–hardware metaphor really do have that distinction in mind. The concept of software is far too broad to help clarify the issues raised in this debate; further detailed specification of what is implied by the term is required.

For a start, use of the term 'software' might be taken to imply the almost certainly misleading view of the visual brain as programmed in something like the way a general purpose digital computer is programmed. That claim is a quite unnecessary one to take on board while trying to defend the view that (even today's) computers and brains are helpfully and properly designated as belonging to a common class of devices, namely, 'Information processors'. IU theories claim that the 'biological visual brain is a computer' only in the sense that it implements computational theories of certain information processing tasks. The question 'Can computers think?' is on this view badly formulated, the answer being 'Yes and no'. A better question is: 'How can this information processing task be solved?' with the follow-up question, once an answer has been offered, 'How can that solution be implemented efficiently in a computer at the algorithm and hardware levels?' Also, given a good computational theory of the task, one can ask whether a biological brain implements it, and use psychophysics and neurophysiology to test various possibilities that the brain might employ in terms of algorithms and hardware.

5.3   *Representational stages and levels of task analysis*

If vision is a hierarchical sequence of representations, it is natural to call the first elements in the hierarchy 'low-level', because they deal with *early visual processing*. A good example of such a representation would be edge points derived from the pixels of the grey level description.

The next layer up, sometimes called *intermediate-level vision*, deals with the properties of surfaces. The 2.5D sketch is the paradigm of this type, although it needs to be remembered that the nature of that representation is currently a research issue and itself almost certainly comprises many layers.

Finally, we can speak of *high-level representations* which make explicit objects present in a scene, their spatial disposition, and such properties as 'grasping points', 'sittable upon', and so on.

If a representation is computed working solely from the data provided by a lower representation in the hierarchy then we speak of *data-driven processing* or *bottom-up processing*. Conversely, if information flows from a higher representation to help resolve ambiguities at a lower level, that process is called *top-down processing*, or sometimes *conceptually driven processing*. Knowledge of the world can be embedded in a visual process in at least two different ways. First, certain processes might use procedures which rely for their effectiveness on some very general assumptions about the 'world out there', such as 'surfaces are generally smooth unless they are viewed at a very short distance'. Processes of that kind utilize implicit knowledge in what is said to be a *procedurally embedded* fashion. On the other hand, processes relying on specific knowledge about specific objects, for example a visual process reasoning that 'this thing could be the eye of a horse in which case that brown hump over there could be its haunches' is using knowledge about a specific object explicitly in a top-down direction.

Marr's approach was to take much more seriously than hitherto an attempt to understand how low-level visual processes can get by without reliance on high-level knowledge about specific objects being 'looked for'. That has not endeared him to many who, perhaps in despair at the poor quality of the images with which they had to work, believed that object recognition relies a great deal on knowledge about what to expect in a scene. Robert's theory described in Part II, Section 7.2, is an example of this kind of theory.

The debate continues, but it should not obscure the fact that Marr's approach, because it is committed root and branch to the business of building scene representations, is nevertheless firmly within the *constructivist* tradition of research on perception. Perhaps the best-known present-day advocate of that tradition is Gregory (e.g. 1980; Part II, p. 109) who promotes the view that 'perception is hypothesis'. Gregory regards our perceptions as the result of our brains considering how data about the world presented by our sense organs can best be 'explained' in terms of stored mental representations. It might be thought that Marr's approach is too 'low-level' to be consistent with Gregory's viewpoint, but I find Marr's work wholly in keeping with the spirit of Gregory's position. Marr's low-level vision theory makes use of general knowledge of the world, building such knowledge into the procedures used to create visual representations. These representations could be regarded as providing 'explanations' of the sensory data and in that sense they could be called 'hypotheses'. Also, it should not be overlooked that, although Marr's low-level vision theory is the best known of his achievements, Marr and Nishihara (1978) provide top-down guidance as a part of their 3D shape matching theory of object recognition.

Because the low-level theories of Marr and his colleagues have taken advantage of the information available in the pattern of light reaching the eyes, their work has sometimes been likened to that of J. J. Gibson (e.g. 1966; Part II, p. 111) who was also concerned with the richness of the *optic array* received by visual receptors. But, despite this similarity, Gibson's rejection of the constructivist viewpoint and his espousal of *direct perception* to my mind places him a long way away from the Image Understanding school. Gibson had little time for those who tried to construct visual representations. Now it is clear that for certain visually guided acts, such as a gull folding its wings as it dives into the sea and needing to judge time to contact, it may be that it is at best strained to talk of constructing a visual representation. It could be (Lee, 1980) that for those sorts of control purposes (which in the human might have their parallel in catching a ball), simple visual parameters are 'directly' computed from the optic flow field impinging on the organism, providing the input needed to trigger wing-folding or hand-closing, without any need for elaborate intermediate surface representations of the approaching seawater or ball.

On the other hand, for the task of picking up an object and manipulating it, it does seem, to this author as well as to the IU community at large, that the construction of a rich set of surface and object representations is required. Not much help has yet come from appeals to direct perception in understanding how to perform such tasks, whatever the success for more automatic processes like wing-folding or ball-catching. The present consensus in IU is that massive computations involving a wide range of representations are needed to extract useful information for guiding object manipulation. The IU challenge to the Gibsonian view is: go and build a visual system that can do such a task and see if you can get by without a rich set of visual representations!

Only time will tell what the answer to that challenge will be. The experience of IU to date has been that what seem like quite simple perceptions, like detecting an edge, turn out to be a lot more complex than at first thought — even more so in the case of being able to pick out, and pick up, recognizable objects. Quite simply, the notion of direct perception is having little impact on present developments in IU, even though some have turned to Gibson's writings for ideas about information available in the optic array impinging on visual receptors. That array is certainly rich in information but whether it can be obtained in usable form given the conceptual framework of 'direct perception' is a moot point. In a series of highly technical sophisticated papers, Koenderink and van Doorn (see 1977 for a review) have provided perhaps the most impressive examination of information in the optic array. For a good discussion of the complexities of the Gibson controversy, consult Ullman (1980) and Bruce and Green (1985), as well as Marr (1982).

Summary of Section 5

- Visual representations consist of a set of syntactic and semantic conventions. The syntactic conventions specify the symbols (primitives) of the representation and the rules for combining them. The semantic conventions specify meanings for the symbols which derive from the use to which they are put in representing the world and providing guidance for actions and for thought.

- It is controversial whether AI computer programs are to be thought of as simulating human processing (weak AI hypothesis) or as replicating it (strong AI hypothesis).

- Marr's work on vision emphasized bottom-up processing but not to the complete exclusion of high-level, and sometimes top-down, processes. It falls within the constructivist tradition, because of its emphasis on building scene representations.

- Gibson's work on direct perception is similar to Marr's approach in as much as they both stress the importance of carefully studying the nature of the incoming information available to the visual system. However, the two approaches contrast strongly over the question of the need for representations. The latter are central to Marr's approach, but they seem to have no place in Gibson's conceptual framework of direct perception.

6   *The future*

It needs to be said once again that the account given here has, for reasons of space, been a brief and highly selective overview of computer vision. The effort being expended on the field as a whole is enormous—which reflects its huge industrial and military potential. This Part has centred on the work of Marr because his contribution has had most to say about the biological vision systems which naturally form the major interest of cognitive psychologists.

The main issues for the immediate future seem to me to be these:

1 Will Marr's recommendations about the general approach required to understand visual systems survive?

Because they are based on a logical analysis of what is required, and because his general arguments seem to me secure, I believe that in a few years' time pretty well everyone will have absorbed them as basic agreed groundwork—and perhaps find it difficult to appreciate what all the fuss was about! But fuss and controversy in abundance is presently the state of the field. Certainly, by no means all neurophysiologists are persuaded that study of the computational problem is the neglected level of analysis (see for example Barlow's recent 1985 Bartlett Memorial Lecture which makes hardly any mention of it). Also, a great deal of effort amongst computer scientists studying vision is concerned with the properties of networks of neuron-like elements. This topic, which has a long history, has recently come back into vogue and is sometimes called *connectionism*. Mayhew and Frisby (1984) provide a review and, despite recognizing the great interest of the field, reiterate Marr's caution that studying algorithms and hardware is not in itself enough. The next few years could provide an interesting unfolding of these issues.

2 One strand of present work that seems highly likely to be of great significance in the near future is that of Koenderink and van Doorn (1977). Their highly technical and sophisticated mathematical treatment of the information available in images was curiously neglected by Marr—and by almost everyone else. Their time seems now to have come, although the number of cognitive psychologists able to grasp the mathematics of what they have to say is probably very limited. This points to a difficulty for those considering a career in the field; it may well be that computer vision will become increasingly a branch of applied mathematics and/or applied physics. Psychologists will undoubtedly have a role to play because they have the expertise to study the best visual system presently known—that of human beings—with all the potential benefit that implies for

understanding how to build good artificial systems. Nevertheless, it may be increasingly difficult for them to make a real contribution—study the right things, ask the right questions—unless they conduct their work within a multi-disciplinary context.

Further reading

1 Mayhew and Frisby (1984). This article provides a more detailed treatment of most of the issues introduced in Part III. It also contains a summary and review of the classic AI vision domain—that of the blocks world.

2 Pollard, Mayhew and Frisby (1985). This paper describes a theory of stereo vision, and a stereo algorithm based upon it. The paper also considers the ways in which the design of the algorithm resembles one of those apparently used by the human vision system, and contrasts it with other stereo algorithms which have been proposed, including the Marr and Poggio algorithm described in Section 3.1.

3 The problem of interpreting disparities to recover the depth values required for a range map has recently been the subject of some new theorizing. This has interesting psychological implications as it turns out that the new theory (Mayhew, 1983; Mayhew and Longuet-Higgins, 1982) explains very neatly a classic binocular depth illusion obtained when one eye's image is magnified in the vertical direction. Frisby (1984) provides a tutorial account of this development.

4 Winston, P. H. (1984) A highly readable general textbook on Artificial Intelligence.

5 Boden, M. (1977) Another highly readable general textbook on Artificial Intelligence.

6 Frisby (1979) A beginner's text on the psychology and neuro-physiology of vision, considered from a computational standpoint.

7 Koenderink and van Doorn (1977). The most approachable of their papers for the non-technical reader.

8 Finally, there is Marr's own book *Vision* (1982). Part I sets out very clearly Marr's philosophical approach to vision and a modified version of Chapter 1 is reprinted in Aitkenhead and Slack (1985). The Epilogue in Part III is also recommended as an entertaining imaginary conversation between Marr and a not-quite-convinced colleague upon whom Marr tries to press his position.

Overview

Ilona Roth

This book has addressed from two main perspectives the question of how we make sense of all the information we receive via the senses. Part I considered the conceptual categories which provide an enduring organization for the knowledge we acquire about the world. Parts II and III had as their main theme more moment-to-moment perceptual experiences of the world. But as the discussion emphasized, these two perspectives are very much interrelated. One of the most important functions of perception is to assign objects to meaningful categories which are stored in memory. This recognition is essential if we are to interact with our surroundings in an efficient way. At the same time, perception provides us with much of the information which we use to form new categories and update old ones. So an object may be recognized or perceptually categorized as a table, while simultaneously furnishing novel features (three legs instead of four) which serve to update the perceiver's stored knowledge of what tables are typically like.

Clearly the potential scope of material to be covered is enormous. In order to reduce this scope to manageable proportions the discussion was limited to the categorization and perception of physical 'things' (two-dimensional patterns, inanimate objects, animals, plants, etc.) and to the visual modality.

Perhaps the most obvious conclusion to emerge from the book is that a variety of complex representations and processes are involved in perception and categorization. Throughout the entire volume, the only theory which has rejected this view has been that of J. J. Gibson. He has argued with some cogency that we can make sense of the visual world without the necessity for complex representations and processes. Yet Marr must speak for many contemporary psychologists in arguing that Gibson has 'missed the point' about the need for processes and representations (see Part II, Section 5). Let us then consider the main types of representations and processes which, according to most psychologists, are involved in categorizing and perceiving things.

Representations for categorizing and perceiving objects

A representation is something that stands for something else. In other words, it is a kind of model of the thing it represents. We have to distinguish between a *representing world* and a *represented world*. The

> representing world must somehow mirror some aspects of the represented world. (Rumelhart and Norman, 1985, p. 16)

In the theories discussed in this book, the represented world is the physical world of patterns and objects, animals, plants etc. Of course, many of the theories have dealt with very limited or simplified aspects of this exceedingly complex world. For instance, experimental studies of perception often employ two-dimensional patterns rather than three-dimensional objects. AI models may be able to cope with three-dimensional objects but these are usually simple geometrical forms. Even Marr's model deals with inputs which are surprisingly like the toy blocks of earlier less sophisticated programs.

Three main classes of 'representing world' have been considered throughout the book:

1 Relatively enduring representations stored in long-term memory.
2 Relatively temporary representations which are constructed as intermediate stages in the processing of sensory input.
3 New representations which are the 'final product' of perceptual processing.

In many ways this is an artificial division, because perception involves a continuous cycle of interaction between all three types of representation. However, it is convenient to divide this cycle into notional parts for purposes of discussion.

1 Representations stored in long-term memory

Part I dealt with several different views of enduring representations. Traditionally, representations for categories such as chair, table, dog, rose, were assumed to consist of lists of features which would define these categories. It was Eleanor Rosch who highlighted the difficulties of defining everyday categories and established the importance of fuzzy representations. Initially, she favoured a version of this position in which everyday categories were assumed to be represented by single composite prototypes based on typical ideas. But she was later forced to acknowledge the role of features, albeit representing what was typical, rather than definitive, about categories. Rosch also stressed the importance of hierarchical relationships in representing conceptual information, arguing that one level in such hierarchies (the basic level) would have special properties as a representation. Like many theoretical dichotomies, the notion that well-defined and fuzzy representations are mutually exclusive alternatives, has inevitably come under attack. Part I concluded by considering the more recent 'dual representation view' according to which many concepts lend themselves to both well-defined and fuzzy types of representation.

In Part I 'enduring' representations were considered in some detail as a dimension of organization in long-term memory. But stored representations also play an important role in processing perceptual inputs. Thus, turning to Part II, even the feature processing hypotheses discussed in Section 3 implicitly assume stored feature representations which are available for matching with features extracted from perceptual inputs.

Other theories discussed in Part II make more explicit assumptions about stored representations. For instance, according to Gregory, perceptual processing is guided by stored representations in the form of unconscious assumptions or hypotheses about the world. We unconsciously assume that a person does not change his size with differences in viewing distance, although the size of the retinal image does. This representation of the world works under normal circumstances, but can occasionally generate illusions. Though this idea of unconscious hypotheses was discussed with reference to size and shape constancy, it can be thought of as a general principle of representation. For instance, a stored list of the most typical features of chairs can be thought of as a hypothesis about what an actual chair is likely to consist of. There is, I think, quite a close affinity between Gregory's notion that our stored representations of the world are hypothetical, and Rosch's idea that they are prototypical. Both ideas allow that an actual perceptual instance may fail to conform to expectations.

Structural descriptions discussed in Part II, Section 6, were developed specifically as a model of the type of representations necessary for perceptual recognition. It may perhaps be worth spelling out the relationship between this and Rosch's representation models discussed in Part I. In many ways the two approaches offer alternative solutions to the problems of traditional feature theories. Very simply, Rosch's approach assumes that for many categories of object, animal, etc., defining characteristics do not exist, only typical ones. In contrast, the structural description model assumes that defining characteristics can be established, provided that one deals with sufficiently complex relationships among features. In essence then, the structural description model assumes that object representations are well defined.

Interestingly, the first of the AI programs discussed in Part II (Roberts' program) uses a representation which combines the well-defined quality of a structural description with the flexibility of a prototype and the inferential function of a hypothesis. The three blocks models (cuboid, wedge, hexagonal cylinder) stored by Roberts' program are in the form of definitions describing the structural relationships among the elements of these blocks. But Roberts called these models 'prototypes' because each serves as a typical example of a category of blocks which can be generated by transforming the prototype. In processing the input from the 'line finder stage' the program adopts as its tentative hypothesis a prototype whose various transformations are tested against input cues.

Turning to Part III it is not surprising to find less mention of the role of stored representations in making sense of input. Marr set out to demonstrate that a good deal of useful information can be extracted from sensory input without guidance from specific stored representations of objects. Nonetheless in handling the problem of how objects are recognized from information in the 2.5D sketch, Marr introduced the idea of stored canonical forms which serve a function very similar to Roberts' prototypes.

2 Intermediate representations of input

The second type of representation dealt with in the book is relatively temporary or intermediate representations of perceptual input. Part I has little to say on this subject. In Part II, we can think of the simple features extracted by feature detection (see Section 3) as temporary representations which are ultimately combined into perceptions of recognizable objects. Perceptual groupings (see Section 4) can also be thought of as a stage in the perception of complex objects and scenes. The most comprehensive treatment of representations as intermediate stages comes in Part III. Marr's basic idea of a sequential series of stages, each of which constitutes a more elaborate version of the input, is by no means new. The beauty of Marr's model lies in the complexity of the information represented in each of his hypothetical stages.

3 New representations of input

Finally, the discussion in this book necessarily assumes that perception produces new representations as a result of processing input. In some ways these new representations of input are the most complex and elusive for a psychologist to describe. If we make a conscious effort to introspect, we become aware of a continuous stream of information about the physical world. We perceive inanimate and animate 'things' each with a specific size, shape, colour and position. We also know the purposes and meanings of all these things. But what are the mental representations which correspond to this awareness? Most of the theories discussed in this book tackle this question only indirectly by specifying some kind of perceptual output which can be measured or described. An output can be anything from the amplitude of response of a single cell in the visual system, to a subject's report that one line in a figure appears longer than the other, to a computer printout describing what blocks are present in a blocks world scene. But most of us must have the feeling that none of these outputs constitutes a perceptual experience in itself. A pitfall which many contemporary theorists have sought to avoid is to assume that perceptual experiences correspond to discrete 'mental objects'. Thus both Marr and Gibson have emphasized the close, if not inextricable, interaction between perception and action.

According to this view recognizing that an object is a table is not so much experiencing a mental picture, as being able to plan what one can do with the object, how to walk round it without collision and so on. This complex association of perceptual and other knowledge may be referred to as a schema (Cohen *et al.*, 1986). Yet this too seems a rather indirect way of describing perceptual experience. There is much scope for research on this issue, but I suspect that some of the answers lie in philosophy rather than in psychology itself.

Processes for categorizing and perceiving objects

One of the most popular ways of describing cognitive processes is to distinguish between those which operate top-down and those which operate bottom-up. Though Part I made no explicit reference to this dichotomy, it did mention the possibility that objects are assigned to categories by feature comparison, which we can assume to operate in a bottom-up direction. But I have already suggested that category representations such as prototypes or typical feature lists may also act as object hypotheses which guide the extraction of sensory information from objects in a top-down fashion.

The bottom-up/top-down distinction was more in evidence in Parts II and III. Part II discussed the inadequacies of traditional feature processing models which operate fairly strictly in a bottom-up fashion. The inferential theories of perception discussed in Section 5 of Part II were in some ways a reaction to the inadequacies of feature models—stressing the need for top-down knowledge about objects to guide the bottom-up processing of input. AI programs such as Roberts' and Waltz's also relied heavily upon stored knowledge to make sense of inputs. It is interesting therefore that Marr's more contemporary approach reinstates bottom-up processing as an efficient way of processing input. The important point to grasp is that though the processing in Marr's model proceeds to a high level without using stored knowledge about what objects are likely to be present in a scene, it *is* guided by general rules about the way the world is organized (e.g. adjacent regions in a scene are likely to belong to the same object; an object cannot be in two places at the same time). One could certainly argue that this information is a kind of knowledge—Frisby refers to it in Part III as 'procedurally embedded knowledge'. It follows therefore that what Marr describes as bottom-up processing is guided by a kind of knowledge, albeit less specific than the object hypotheses assumed by some inferential models. And of course even Marr's program employs, in its final stages, stored information about objects, referred to as 'canonical forms'. In general, the distinction between top-down and bottom-up processing should be treated as one of degree rather than kind.

A similar point applies to some other 'processing dichotomies' which were introduced in Part II. For instance a distinction was drawn between local-to-global processing and global-to-local processing. Yet there are certainly cases in which, to achieve a meaningful result, information must flow simultaneously in both directions. Another rather fuzzy distinction is between 'automatic' and 'consciously-controlled' processing. Many of the processes discussed in this book appear to occur outside our conscious control. We cannot really choose whether we see a visual illusion, just as we cannot choose to see a complex object, such as a chair, as a number of disconnected parts. Yet this kind of control may be achieved with practice. An artist may consciously select an unconventional perception of a scene, even achieving the kind of 'pointillist' representation which, according to Marr's model, is an early stage in visual processing. Finally, the discussion has highlighted the theoretical interdependency of 'direct' perception and other more 'constructivist' models. Direct perception certainly does not seem viable as a comprehensive model of perception. But it has served as a useful corrective to the view that complex information cannot be extracted by the early stages in processing input.

Answers to SAQs

SAQ 1

(a) The list of properties is not sufficient for the category 'square' because it applies not only to squares but to other four-sided figures such as rectangles and parallelograms. Thus a figure which possesses this list of properties is not *guaranteed* to be a member of the category 'square'.

(b) If we add the properties 'All sides are equal' and 'All angles are 90°' the description becomes necessary and sufficient for the category 'square', i.e. any figure possessing the properties is guaranteed to be a square.

SAQ 2

(a) and (b) are properties which an object must have to be a chair.

SAQ 3

The combination of properties applies to several items of furniture including seats, benches and sofas. It is interesting to note that the *Oxford English Dictionary* gives 'for one person to sit on' as a characteristic of chairs. If we add this to my list of properties, it certainly narrows the range of objects to which the description applies. Yet there are still some non-chairs (e.g. bar stools) which possess all the properties on the list, so it still fails as a clear-cut definition. Notice too that few people think of this particular property when listing the properties they associate with chairs.

SAQ 4

(i) My description for 'dog' is as follows:
   (a) Animal
   (b) Household pet
   (c) Has four legs
   (d) Has a tail
   (e) Has a hairy coat
   (f) Barks
   (g) Eats meat

(ii) (a) is a property which all dogs must have to be dogs—so it is necessary. (c), (d) and (e) look at first sight like necessary properties. However, notice that a dog which has lost a leg or tail in an accident, or has lost its hair through illness, is still recognizably a dog. So these are only necessary properties 'under normal circumstances'. It is precisely this kind of qualifying clause which has led many philosophers to reject the notion of necessary properties for this kind of category. (b), (f) and (g) are all properties which some dogs genuinely lack, so they are not necessary either.

(iii) There is probably no combination of properties on my list which applies only to dogs. Items (a) to (e) apply to many mammals besides dogs. Even if we include items (f) and (g) we have a description which could apply to a pet fox! Thus, unlike our list for 'triangle', the list of items does not constitute a clear-cut definition of the category 'dog'. However, it certainly applies to most dogs and to few other categories.

(iv) As a zoologist one might draw up a list of more technical properties, such as vertebrate, mammal, carnivorous. In this way, it is possible to produce a pretty clear specification of the category, which looks much like a set of necessary and sufficient properties. However, many contemporary zoologists would argue that absolute definition is impossible for biological categories. As we noted earlier, the living world is made up of attributes 'clustered together' to form natural discontinuities — but these clusters are not perfect. The living world is full of evolutionary exceptions — organisms which are on the borderline between one category and another. For further discussion of the principles of scientific classification see the articles listed under further reading.

SAQ 5
(a) Attributes are Shading and Shape
 Values are Plain and Square.
(b) The items to which the rule 'Plain Squares' applies are: 3, 12, 21.

SAQ 6
(a) Since card 16 has two crosses and card 7 has one, the attribute which has changed its value is number of shapes.
(b) If the E says 7 is a positive instance of the rule, this means that the rule still applies despite changing the number of shapes from two to one. It can be concluded that the number of shapes attribute is irrelevant — i.e. not part of the rule.
(c) If the E says 7 is not an instance, this means that the rule no longer applies when the number of shapes is changed from two to one. It can be concluded that the number of shapes attribute is relevant — i.e. is part of the rule.

SAQ 7
(a) Since item 13 has two crosses the S can conclude that his hypothesis (the rule is 'two crosses') is tenable. A subject operating strictly on a hypothesis testing strategy might go on to seek further confirming instances. However, a subject who noticed that the shading attribute had been eliminated would realize that logically 'two crosses' must be the correct rule.
(b) Since item 13 has two crosses, the S must conclude that his hypothesis (the rule is two crosses) is incorrect, and he should select another rule to test. Notice that a negative instance can be just as informative to the S as a positive instance.
(c) Item 14 is one to which the rule 'two crosses' does not apply. The fact that it is negative is still consistent with 'two crosses' being the rule. The S should conclude that his rule may be correct and should go on testing.

SAQ 8
Different cultures have different culinary habits. For instance, 'squash' is a widely used vegetable in the USA, but not in this country, so we would expect Americans to give it a higher typicality rating than British people. Obviously availability of squash is a factor, but there is no evidence that the familiarity or frequency of the word 'squash' in our language affects its typicality rating.

SAQ 9
According to the typicality ratings given in Table 2, 'chair' has a higher rating than 'rug' so should be categorized faster. Similarly, in Table 3, 'carrot' has a higher typicality rating than 'mushroom', so should be categorized faster.

SAQ 10
According to the number of attributes they share with potato, the order of rated typicality for the three vegetables should be:

     Carrot   Corn   Peanut

Notice that in Table 3, which was taken from Rosch, potato has a lower typicality rating than the other three vegetables whereas in this study using British Ss it has a higher rating. This is another example of how culture affects typicality ratings.

SAQ 11
(a) The relative cue validity for the three features is

      Feathers   (Most)
      Flies
      Brown colour   (Least)

'Feathers' would be the most useful feature in deciding whether an entity was a bird, because it is usually associated with birds and rarely associated with other concepts. 'Brown colour' would be the least useful because though quite a few birds are brown, so are many other animals and other objects; similarly there are quite a few birds which are *not* brown. 'Flying' is quite distinctive, but is also a feature of some mammals, aeroplanes, angels, etc.!
(b) Each of the birds has two of the three features on the above list. But 'parrot' has the more highly weighted combination of features ('feathers' and 'flies'), whereas 'emu' has the less highly weighted combination ('feathers' and 'brown colour').

SAQ 12
According to Berlin's findings, the intermediate level shown in Figure 1.9 should be basic for birds. The intermediate level categories also seem (to be at least) the most distinctive and coherent for the furniture hierarchy.

SAQ 13
Since light in the 'on-centre' of the field produces increased activity, whereas light in the 'off-surround' produces decreased activity, these opposing responses should cancel each other out when light is presented to both areas simultaneously. Actual recordings from such cells usually indicate no net change in the resting activity when a diffuse light covering the whole receptive field is presented. This is just one example of the retina's role in transmitting the information which the organism needs and filtering out insignificant information (a small compact fluctuating light source is more likely to signify part of an object than a large diffuse light source).

SAQ 14
(a) Letters such as G, O and Q, which share several features with C.
(b) An N would be easily located in an array of letters such as O, P, Q and S, with which it shares few features in common.

SAQ 15
A square seems the 'best' and 'simplest' organization of the four dots, and therefore conforms to the Law of Pragnanz. Most people should actually report seeing the figure as a square.

SAQ 16
Hierarchical feature analysis is local-to-global because it commences with local features and builds up progressively to an interpretation of a whole pattern.

SAQ 17
There are two main possibilities. One is that constancy scaling does not work over quite such long distances. The other is that the visual cues for depth are absent when we look down on a scene through a relatively empty space.

Answers to SAQs

SAQ 18
According to Gregory's theory texture gradients would act as cues from which depth or distance is inferred, rather than specifying depth directly in the optic array.

SAQ 19
For b — vertical line with closed loop attached at the bottom right.
For d — vertical line with closed loop attached at the bottom left.
For p — vertical line with closed loop attached at the top right.

SAQ 20
The results in Figure 2.22 suggest that most Ss are using the first structural description. There were 66 correct responses for the diamond shape, which is part of this description, but only 11 for the parallelogram, which is part of the second description.

SAQ 21
Only the third description applies to both of the line drawings.

SAQ 22
The square is a cue for the hexagonal cylinder. The triangle is a cue for a wedge.

SAQ 23
The final output of the program is object-centred. Since the program can identify the blocks, and produce alternative views of them, the output is not specific to one particular view of the blocks.

SAQ 24
This program works bottom-up, because the interpretations of line junction cues are not guided by specific hypotheses about what the objects in the scene might be. Instead these interpretations are based on set rules about which parts of the input should be linked together, given the cues. Notice, however, that these rules do constitute a type of knowledge. This suggests that the distinction between top-down and bottom-up processing is not a clear-cut dichotomy between processes which are guided by knowledge and those which are not. It is the *nature* of the knowledge which is important.

References

AITKENHEAD, A. M. and SLACK, J. M. (eds) (1985) *Issues in Cognitive Modeling*, Lawrence Erlbaum Associates.

ARMSTRONG, S. L., GLEITMAN, L. R. and GLEITMAN, H. (1983) 'What some concepts might not be', *Cognition*, 13, pp. 263–308; reprinted in Aitkenhead and Slack (eds) (1985) pp. 101–129.

ATRAN, S. (1985) 'Constraints on the semantics of living kinds: a commonsense alternative to recent treatments of natural-object terms', unpublished paper.

BARLOW, H., BLAKEMORE, C. and PETTIGREW, J. D. (1967) 'The neural mechanism of binocular depth discrimination', *Journal of Physiology (London)*, 193, pp. 327–42.

BERLIN, B. (1972) 'Speculations on the growth of ethno-botanical nomenclature', *Language in Society*, 1, pp. 51–86.

BLAKEMORE, C. (1973) 'The baffled brain' in R. L. Gregory and E. G. Gombrich, (eds), *Illusion in Nature and Art*, Duckworth.

BODEN, M. (1977) *Artificial Intelligence and Natural Man*, Harvester Press.

BROOKS, R. A. (1981) 'Symbolic reasoning among 3D models and 2D images', *Artificial Intelligence*, 17, pp. 285–348.

BRUCE, V. and GREEN, P. (1985) *Visual Perception: Physiology, Psychology and Ecology*, Lawrence Erlbaum Associates.

BRUNER, J. S., GOODNOW, J. J. and AUSTIN, J. G. (1956) *A Study of Thinking*, Wiley.

CARELMAN, J. (1971) *Catalogue of Extraordinary Objects* (translated by Rosaleen Walsh) Abelard-Schuman.

CLOWES, M. B. (1971) 'On seeing things', *Artificial Intelligence*, 2 pp. 79–116.

COHEN, G., EYSENCK, M. W. and LE VOI, M. E. (1986) *Memory: a Cognitive Approach*, Open University Press (Open Guides to Psychology series).

COLLINS, A. and QUILLIAN, M. R. (1969) 'Retrieval time from semantic memory', *Journal of Verbal Learning and Verbal Behaviour*, 8, pp. 240–47.

CONWAY, M. (1984) 'Content and organizational differences between autobiographical and semantic memories', Human Cognition Research Laboratory, Open University, Technical Report No. 7.

FREYD, J. J. (1983) 'Shareability: the social psychology of epistemology', *Cognition*, 7.

FRISBY, J. P. (1979) *Seeing: Illusion, Brain and Mind*, Oxford University Press.

FRISBY, J. P. (1984) 'An old illusion and a new theory of stereoscopic depth perception', *Nature*, Vol. 307, No. 5952, pp. 592–3.

GIBSON, E. (1969) *Principles of Perceptual Learning and Development*, Appleton-Century-Crofts.

GIBSON, J. J. (1966) *The Scenes Considered as Perceptual Systems*, Houghton Mifflin.

GIBSON, J. J. (1979) *The Ecological Approach to Visual Perception*, Houghton-Mifflin.

GREENE, J. (1986) *Language: A Cognitive Approach*, Open University Press (Open Guides to Psychology series).

References

GREGORY, R. L. (1973) 'The confounded eye', in R. L. Gregory and E. H. Gombrich (eds). *Illusion in Nature and Art*, Duckworth.

GREGORY, R. L. (1980) 'Perceptions as hypotheses', *Philosophical Transactions of the Royal Society of London*, Series B, 290, pp. 181–97.

GREGORY, R. L. and GOMBRICH, E. H. (eds) (1973) *Illusion in Nature and Art*, Duckworth.

GUZMAN, A. (1969) 'Decomposition of a visual scene into three dimensional bodies', in A. Grasselli (ed.) *Automatic Interpretation and Classification of Images*, Academic Press.

HABER, R. N. and HERSHENSON, M. (1973) *The Psychology of Visual Perception*, Holt, Rinehart and Winston.

HUBEL, D. H. and WIESEL, T. N. (1959) 'Receptive fields of single neurones in the cat's striate cortex', *Journal of Physiology*, 148, pp. 574–91.

HUBEL, D. H. and WIESEL, T. N. (1962) 'Receptive fields, binocular interaction and functional architecture in the cat's visual cortex', *Journal of Physiology (London)*, 16, pp. 106–154.

HUFFMAN, D. A. (1971) 'Impossible objects and nonsense sentences', in B. Meltzer and D. Michie (eds) *Machine Intelligence* 6, Edinburgh University Press.

JOHNSON-LAIRD, P. N., HERRMANN, D. J. and CHAFFIN, R. (1984) 'Only connections: a critique of semantic networks', *Psychological Bulletin*, Vol. 96, No. 2, pp. 292–315.

JOHNSON-LAIRD, P. N. and WASON, P. C. (1977) *Thinking: Readings in Cognitive Science*, Cambridge University Press.

JULESZ, B. (1971) *Foundations of Cyclopean Perception*, University of Chicago Press.

JULESZ, B. (1981) 'Textons, the elements of texture perception and their interactions', *Nature*, 290, pp. 91–7.

JULESZ, B. and FRISBY, J. P. (1975) 'Some new subjective contours in random-line stereograms', *Perception,* 4, pp. 145–50.

KOENDERINK, J. J. and VAN DOORN, A. J. (1977) 'How an ambulant observer can construct a model of the environment from the geometrical structure of the visual inflow' in G. Hauske and E. Butenandt (eds), *Kybernetik 1977*, pp. 224–47, Oldenburg.

KOFFKA, K. (1935) *Principles of Gestalt Psychology*, Harcourt Brace Jovanovich.

KOSSLYN, S. M. (1985) 'The medium and the message in mental imagery: a theory' in Aitkenhead and Slack (eds) (1985).

KUFFLER, S. W. (1953) 'Discharge patterns and functional organisation of mammalian retina', *Journal of Neurophysiology*, 16, pp. 37–68.

LABOV, W. (1973) 'The boundaries of words and their meanings', in C. J. Bailey and R. Shuy (eds), *New Ways of Analysing Variations in English*, Georgetown University Press.

LEACH, E. (1964) 'Anthropological aspects of language: animal categories and verbal abuse', in E. H. Lenneberg, *New Directions in the Study of Language*, Massachusetts Institute of Technology Press.

LEE, D. N. (1980) 'The optic flow field: the foundation of vision', in H. C. Longuet-Higgins and N. S. Sutherland (eds) *The Psychology of Vision*, pp. 169–78.

LUPKER, S. J. (1979) 'On the nature of perceptual information during letter perception', *Perception and Psychophysics*, 25, pp. 303–312.

MARR, D. (1976) 'Early processing of visual information', *Philosophical Transactions of the Royal Society of London*, Series B, 275, pp. 483–524.

MARR, D. (1982) *Vision*, W. H. Freeman.

MARR, D. (1985) 'Vision: the philosophy and the approach' in A. M. Aitkenhead and J. M. Slack (eds) (1985) pp. 133–56.

MARR, D. and HILDRETH, E. (1980) 'Theory of edge detection', *Proceedings of the Royal Society of London*, Series B, 207, pp. 187–217.

MARR, D. and NISHIHARA, H. K. (1978) 'Representation and recognition of the spatial organization of three-dimensional shapes', *Proceedings of the Royal Society of London*, Series B, 200, pp. 269–94.

MARR, D. and POGGIO, T. (1976) 'Cooperative computation of stereo disparity', *Science*, 194, pp. 283–7.

MARR, D. and POGGIO, T. (1979) 'A computational theory of human stereo vision', *Proceedings of the Royal Society of London*, Series B, 204, pp. 301–328.

MAYHEW, J. E. W. (1983) 'The interpretation of stereo-disparity information: the computation of surface orientation and depth', *Perception*, 11, pp. 387–403.

MAYHEW, J. E. W. and FRISBY, J. P. (1981) 'Psychophysical and computational studies towards a theory of human stereopsis', *Artificial Intelligence*, 17, pp. 349–85.

MAYHEW, J. E. W. and FRISBY, J. P. (1984) 'Computer vision' in T. O'Shea and M. Eisenstadt (eds) *Artificial Intelligence: Tools, Techniques, and Applications*, Harper and Row, pp. 301–57.

MAYHEW, J. E. W. and LONGUET-HIGGINS, H. C. (1982) 'A computational model of binocular depth perception', *Nature*, 297, pp. 376–9.

MERVIS, C. B. and ROSCH, E. (1981) 'Categorization of natural objects', *Annual Review of Psychology*, 32, pp. 89–115.

MEYER, D. E. SCHVANEVELDT, R. W. and RUDDY, W. G. (1975) 'Loci of contextual effects on visual word recognition', in P. M. A. Rabbitt and S. Dornic (eds) *Attention and Performance*, Academic Press.

MURPHY, G. L. and WRIGHT, J. C. (1984) 'Changes in conceptual structure with expertise: differences between real-world experts and novices', *Journal of Experimental Psychology: Learning Memory and Cognition*, Vol. 10, No. 1, pp. 144–55.

NAVON, D. (1977) 'Forest before trees: the precedence of global features in visual perception', *Cognitive Psychology*, 9, pp. 353–83.

NEISSER, U. (1963) 'Decision-time without reaction-time: experiments in visual scanning', *American Journal of Psychology*, 75, pp. 376–85.

OATLEY, K. (1972) *Brain Mechanisms and Mind*, Thames and Hudson.

OLSON, R. K. and ATTNEAVE, F. (1970) 'What variables produce similarity grouping?', *American Journal of Psychology*, 83, pp. 1–21.

PALMER, S. E. (1975) 'The effects of contextual scenes on the identification of objects', *Memory and Cognition*, 3, pp. 519–26.

PERRETT, D. I. *et al.* (1985) 'Visual cells in the temporal cortex sensitive to face view and gaze direction', *Proceedings of the Royal Society of London*, Series B, pp. 293–317.

POGGIO, G. F. and POGGIO, T. (1984) 'The analysis of stereopsis', *Annual Review of Neuroscience*, 7, pp. 379–412.

POLLARD, S. MAYHEW, J. E. W. and FRISBY, J. P. (1985) 'A stereo correspondence algorithm using a disparity gradient limit', *Perception* (in press).

References

POMERANTZ, J. R. (1981) 'Perceptual organization in information processing' in A. M. Aitkenhead and J. M. Slack (eds) (1985) pp. 157–88.

POMERANTZ, J. R. and GARNER, W. R. (1973) 'Stimulus configuration in selective attention tasks', *Perception and Psychophysics*, 14, pp. 565–9.

POMERANTZ, J. R. and SCHWAITZBERG, S. D. (1975) 'Grouping by proximity: selective attention measures', *Perception and Psychophysics*, 18, pp. 355–61.

REED, S. K. (1973) *Psychological Processes in Pattern Recognition*, Academic Press.

REED, S. K. (1974) 'Structural descriptions and the limitations of visual images', *Memory and Cognition*, 2, pp. 329–36.

ROBERTS, L. G. (1965) 'Machine perception of three-dimensional solids', In J. T. Tippett, D. A. Berkowitz, L. C. Clapp, C. J. Koester and A. Vanderburgh (eds), *Optical and Electro-optical Information Processing*, Massachusetts Institute of Technology Press.

ROSCH, E. (1973) 'On the internal structure of perceptual and semantic categories', in T. E. Moore (ed) *Cognitive Development and the Acquisition of Language*, Academic Press.

ROSCH, E. (1975) 'Cognitive representations of semantic categories', *Journal of Experimental Psychology: General*, Vol. 104, No. 3, pp. 192–233.

ROSCH, E. and MERVIS, C. B. (1975) 'Family resemblance studies in the internal structure of categories', *Cognitive Psychology*, 7, pp. 573–605.

ROSCH, E. MERVIS, C. B., GRAY, W. D., JOHNSON, D. M. and BOYES-GRAEM, P. (1976) 'Basic objects in natural categories', *Cognitive Psychology*, 8, pp. 382–439.

RUMELHART, D. (1977) *Introduction to Human Information Processing*, Wiley.

RUMELHART, D. E. and NORMAN, D. A. (1985) 'Representation of knowledge' in Aitkenhead and Slack (eds) (1985).

SEARLE, J. (1984) *Minds, Brains and Science*, BBC Reith Lectures 1984. Listener (reproduced in *The Listener*).

SLOMAN, A. (1980) *The Computer Revolution in Philosophy*, Harvester Press and Humanities Press.

SMITH, E. E. and MEDIN, D. L. (1981) *Categories and Concepts*, Harvard University Press.

SUTHERLAND, N. S. (1973) 'Object recognition', in Carterette, E. and Friedman, M. (eds) *Handbook of Perception, vol.3: Biology of perceptual systems*, Academic Press.

ULLMAN, S. (1980) 'Against direct perception', *Behavioural and Brain Sciences*, 3, pp. 373–415.

WALTZ, D. L. (1975) 'Generating semantic descriptions from scenes with shadows' in P. H. Winston (ed) *The Psychology of Computer Vision*, McGraw-Hill.

WINSTON, P. H. (1984) *Artificial Intelligence*, Addison-Wesley.

Index of Authors

Index of Authors

Index of Concepts

Index of Concepts